BUSINE

In the same series

*General & Social Letter Writing
*Your Business, The Right Way To Run It
Book-Keeping The Right Way
Microcomputers For Business & Home
The Right Way To Apply For A Job
The Right Way To Write Your Own C.V.

Uniform with this book
**By the same author*

BUSINESS LETTERS

by

Andrew George Elliot

PAPERFRONTS
ELLIOT RIGHT WAY BOOKS
KINGSWOOD, SURREY, U.K.

Typeset in 10/12pt Times
by County Typesetters, Margate, Kent.

Made and Printed in Great Britain by
Richard Clay Ltd., Bungay, Suffolk.

CONTENTS

INTRODUCTION

With the growth of world trade and the need for Britain to export more, business correspondence remains vitally important.

In recent years the standard of grammar and the setting out of letters have improved but I regret to say the contents or ingredients still need attention.

Large amounts of money are being spent on management education and business courses, leading to a flow of trained business managers coming steadily onto the market. More letters neatly typed in better English seem to be the sole result. It's not good enough. A well typed, grammatically correct letter, without the *body* or *meat* which *matters*, is a trifling reward for all this expenditure. The colleges ought to be teaching good letter writing.

Few people can write an exciting and informative letter which adequately deals with the subject or anticipates the questions likely to arise in the recipient's mind. This deficiency, which applies so widely, results largely from the common human failing of being unable to put oneself in the other person's place.

This branch of the subject is the essence of my book and if I have stimulated your imagination I shall be delighted. Any fool can write a letter; it takes a wise man to write a good one

– a letter that can make its message clear, and bring home to the recipient all the information he is entitled to expect; in a word a competent letter.

1

GENERAL REMARKS

Napoleon is reputed to have remarked that every unanswered letter eventually answers itself, and no doubt there are still a certain number of "Napoleons" in existence, particularly in large organisations; but so far as getting on in business is concerned, I think they will all end in the same way – in disaster.

There are a number of books available on letter writing, but unfortunately many of them are still advocating methods which may have been acceptable in the leisurely days of old but are outdated by the accelerated pace of modern commercial life.

It may here be helpful to examine certain elementary rules applicable to letter writing. First, their purpose is to convey information and this should be done in the fewest possible words consistent with clarity and courtesy. Replies to letters and enquiries should, if possible, normally be sent by return; failing this, a postcard should be dispatched immediately, acknowledging the correspondence and promising an early answer or indicating when one will be sent. Sending a brief card or letter to acknowledge the receipt of an important letter will give you time to think carefully about your reply. Where delay is possible, never under-estimate the importance of a day or more's consideration before posting any correspondence which may have serious repercussions. Frequently this will result in the re-writing of the letter or perhaps its cancellation.

Second, always try to put yourself in the place of the recipient to make sure your letter is clear, courteous and avoids annoying the receiver unless, of course, that is your deliberate intention. On this point, I believe that of every one hundred people who write letters to get their own back or to annoy, ninety-nine later regret having done so.

Letter Headings

These should contain the name of the company or organisation, its place of registration, registered number and the address of its registered office (if different from the heading), directors' names, the post code, telephone number(s), telegraphic address and telex and fax numbers.

Under the 1981 Companies Act all business owners in Great Britain who trade under a name other than their own are required to display their own real names and addresses on their business stationery (which includes business letters, written orders for the supply of goods or services, invoices and receipts issued in the course of the business and written demands for payment of debts arising in the course of the business).

INDIVIDUALS

This Act applies to an individual whose business is known as "A. Smith Bakery" even though his own name may be A. Smith. But it does not apply to him if his business is known as "A. Smith" or just simply "Smith". A married woman who is usually known by her married name yet conducts her business using her maiden name must also conform with the Act.

PARTNERSHIPS

If a partnership exists between certain types of companies or a combination of individuals and such companies and they do not trade under their true or corporate name then they must comply with the Act. For example: "Brown & Smith Building Merchants" and "Smith Beauty Products & Brown" (where the true name of "Smith Beauty Products" is "Smith Beauty Products Limited").

However, if a partnership is made up of twenty or more partners then the names of the partners do not have to be included on all business documents, provided that such documents give the address of the main place of business and that a full list of the partners' names and addresses may be seen there.

COMPANIES

If "XYZ Meats (Great Britain) Limited" trades as "XYZ Meats", then the company will have to comply with this Act. As would a limited company that purchased "Ye Olde Inn" but retained this business name.

This law also applies to all companies capable of being wound up under the Companies Act, which includes unregistered companies and overseas companies as defined in Sections 398 and 406 of the Companies Act 1948.

STYLES OF LETTER HEADINGS

A business with wide contacts with the public, or with many new customers, benefits by creating a good first impression. Many firms like to use a colophon or emblem, which can look attractive on the notepaper, and you may choose to do this.

Letter headings may also be die-stamped or embossed, but as these methods cost more, most companies now use a cheaper style and forgo the elegance for economy. Some people like a simple basic style of heading which gives the impression of dependability, whilst others prefer a more modern design. Remember to choose a style which will suit you and your profession or trade; a loud letter head would hardly do for a consultant surgeon.

A few firms use advertising matter in their letter headings and there is no special reason against this. Some firms might have a photograph of one of their products or of their shop or factory. Another firm might wish to put line drawings of several of their products, perhaps down the side of their letter heading. Again, many might wish to give a list of their products. All this, however, is somewhat beyond the scope of our book, except to say that unless it is very well done it can look a mess. So if you are going in for this type of advertising on your letter heading, be sure to ask your printer's co-operation in the layout. If he has not got an art department it may mean employing a local advertising agent or studio. The point to remember is that these people can be very expensive so it is wise to enquire about the cost first.

One important point to bear in mind is to choose a type style that is easy to read and not too small (especially for telephone numbers). It is better if letter headings are not printed smaller than "10 point" capital type (to the layman that means the letter should be a minimum of just under 3mm/⅛″ deep) as then all the important information can be obtained at a glance.

For appearance and economy of space however, the heading should not occupy more than approximately 5cm/2″ of an A4 page, otherwise insufficient space is left for the letter itself. Frequently about 2.5cm/1″ is enough, whilst for half-sheets 2cm/¾″ may suffice. Also, if the name and address occupy a centralised position, less space is sacrificed – an important consideration for half or small sheets of note-paper.

I personally prefer to see commas used to separate the different parts of an address on headed notepaper as I think this makes the address easier to read. For example, if the

THWAITE

DIRECTORS: T. W. THWAITE, A. R. THWAITE, SIR HENRY SMALLSHAW Bt.
Registered in England
No. 317902

A. W. THWAITE AND SONS LTD.,
46–8 NEW MARKET, BIRMINGHAM B5 4AX
Telephone: 021-643 2032 Telex: Thwaite Birmingham 60291
BRANCHES: LONDON, BRISTOL, PRESTON

OUR REF. **YOUR REF.**

Here is an example of a very modern layout featuring narrow horizontal lines. The name of the company is boldly placed to stand out well at the top left and may be printed in a different colour.

GILL

A. R. Gill and Son,

41-51 Westbury Road,

London, WC1 9AB

01-826 1129

A dynamic and go-ahead layout particularly suitable for short names, very simple and much improved by printing the main name in red or some other colour.

Thistle Limited
46 Dean Wells Street
London EC1 2AZ

Export Department
Telephone
01-248 0132

THISTLE

Elliot Right Way Books
Kingswood Buildings,
Kingswood, Surrey, KT20 6TD

6th January 19

fh/674

Dear Sirs,

Another attractive modern style with horizontal lines. A colophon is featured to add impact and therefore the name is in smaller type. The names of the directors should appear at the bottom of the page; this gives the whole page a balanced aspect.

address was 222 Downs Way North Newington, it would not be clear (particularly to a foreigner) whether the correct address was 222 Downs Way, North Newington, or 222 Downs Way North, Newington.

Coloured inks can be used either on the letter heading or for the contents, but black is still frequently used.

Some firms, such as mail order businesses, find that when they make a major alteration in the layout of their headings, or change the colours and design, this attracts new business, and is therefore worth the extra cost. It is only fair to add that in many trades it probably makes no difference.

A business may be well advised to include in its letter heading the statement: "Goods offered subject to prior sale and confirmation", as this affords some protection against errors in quotations.

The layout for letter headings can, as a rule, safely be left to an experienced printer unless you have any preference, which should be indicated in your copy or verbally. He should be requested to use a clear, bold type, and submit proofs for your approval on the paper to be used for the job.

Stationery

For suitable sizes of notepaper it will be found that general business needs are met by the metric international size A4 sheets (210mm x 297mm/11¾" x 8¼") and A5 sheets (148mm x 210mm/8¼" x 5⅞").

A common and good practice is to include a square or oblong for the reference. This brings the reference to notice and, suitably placed, acts as a guide to the typist in setting the margin, giving the letter a balanced, neat effect.

Similarly, a special space can be set aside for the recipient's address. This is often the practice when the letter is to be sent in a window envelope. The corners of the space can be marked as a guide for the typist or the whole space can be enclosed by a box.

A stock of continuation sheets, headed only by the firm's name and the word "Continuation", can be carried if any long letters are anticipated, or plain paper can be used instead, but one usually finds that most letters can be typed on a single page.

In large organisations where different departments need a copy of any relevant correspondence, sheets of varying colours may be used for the different copies. But in smaller companies, plain white paper is quite acceptable.

Chairmen of large companies often have their own special notepaper and heading; when this is done, it is normal to use an expensive paper, often a grey or blue tinted paper. Any good printer can advise on this.

For firms doing overseas business, a supply of specially thin and light-weight air mail letter headings may be required. A neatly printed air letter heading is much more attractive and imposing than the old-fashioned method of stamping your firm's name and address onto the paper.

ENVELOPES

The type and size of envelopes used are a matter of taste, although metric-sized envelopes are generally used to match metric-sized paper. Some wealthy organisations will have tinted notepaper and envelopes to match; others may have definite views about the size of their envelopes; they may, for instance, prefer the square to the oblong size for general use.

It is also a useful precaution to have all envelopes stamped or printed with the sender's name and address on the flap, or, for larger envelopes, on the left-hand corner of the face. This is naturally of assistance to the Post Office – and may also serve the additional purpose of dissuading employees from using business stationery for their personal correspondence.

It helps the Post Office if you use the Post Office Preferred (P.O.P.) range of envelopes and cards. To fall within the P.O.P. range, envelopes should be at least 90mm x 140mm and not larger than 120mm x 235mm.

ACKNOWLEDGEMENTS

If yours is a business which is of small or medium size, acknowledgements can be sent on an ordinary A5 letter heading, but if you have a business which receives many letters it would pay you to have either:-

(a) Postcards already printed with wording such as:

"Dear Sir(s) or Madam,

I/We thank you for your letter of ....
and hope to reply fully in a few days."

Or (b) An A5 letter already printed, on similar lines to (a) above.

Or (c) Instead of having the postcards or letters actually printed, you could type out the basic wording onto appropriate-sized paper or card and use a photocopier to produce the required number of copies, or keep it in the memory of a word processor.

With staff costs soaring and competition severe, it is usually wise to make use of the latest office equipment to produce these time-saving methods.

Of course if your business requires only the occasional copy of some document you will not need to have a photocopying machine on your own premises. Instead it will be cheaper for you just to visit one of the many shops in our high streets which provide such a photocopying service.

OFFICE FORMS

One can save an enormous amount of time and therefore money by having systems worked out to meet recurring conditions. Many successful firms have been doing this for years.

Standard forms can be used for giving quotations to customers, for example:

Thank you for your enquiry of .... We have much pleasure in quoting as follows:

....

....

They can also be used for advice notes, with wording perhaps like this:

Our representative, Mr John W Hall, will have much pleasure in calling upon you at .... a.m. on ....

On page 20 is another form, which happens to be applicable to our business.

Your trade or industry will require different wordings and while one does not want to go "form mad", by thinking and planning you can save much time and effort. We have worked out forms for contracts, placing orders and enquiries as well as a mass of office forms.

It is usually impossible to depend on the required forms to be found in the shops, as the wording rarely fits in with individual needs.

As with the acknowledgements, these forms can either be printed specially or photocopied when required, with the relevant figures, dates, etc. being filled in, and/or the appropriate boxes being crossed or ticked where applicable. Another alternative is to store the basic information and layout in the memory of a word processor/computer and just print out the sections which apply to the particular correspondent.

Preparing your own forms as required is certainly time well spent.

ELLIOT RIGHT WAY BOOKS

(Directors: A. C. Elliot, M. G. Elliot Registered in England No. 813524)

KINGSWOOD BUILDINGS, LOWER KINGSWOOD, TADWORTH, SURREY, KT20 6TD, U.K.

MOGADOR (STD 0737) 832202

Name: ....

Address: ....

....

Thank you for your order. Please return this form with your reply to save delay.

The item marked ☒ is applicable to you.

☐ This book is out-of-print so is no longer available.

☐ Your letter contained no money. Perhaps you overlooked it. The envelope was shut. Please send cheque/P.O. and we will despatch.

☐ The book(s) you enquired about is/are available. Please send cheque/P.O. and we will despatch.

☐ We do not accept credit card sales since we are not retailers.

☐ Your cheque is not negotiable because it is unsigned/out-of-date/words disagree with figures. Please correct, initialling any alteration, or send a new cheque, and we will despatch.

☐ You do not say which book(s) you require, please give details.

Memoranda

These forms are used for inter-office communication. They are often headed as follows:

MEMORANDUM

FROM:	REF:
TO:	DATE:
SUBJECT:	

The text is then typed without further preamble.

Digests and Précis

A digest merely means a summary and is often drawn up for the benefit of busy executives or officials who have not the time to devote to reading through long texts or reports. Although its importance lies in its being short, nothing of value must be omitted; niceties of style and all extraneous matter must be eliminated for word economy, so that the reader is in possession of all the salient facts and sufficient of the original text or report to enable him to grasp it thoroughly.

A *précis* is a French word meaning "summary" or "abstract".

2

ELEMENTARY GRAMMAR AND PUNCTUATION

Grammar

Grammar is to many a rather terrifying subject and for this reason it is apt to assume an importance out of all proportion to its purpose.

It is true that many colloquialisms used in everyday speech are ungrammatical but they are accepted, and indeed, if our grammar were consistently accurate in speech we would be regarded by our more fallible fellow beings as *poseurs* and pedants. It is fortunately true that *sound* will often prove an invaluable guide to the written word.

The ordinary businessman need not be unduly anxious about the way he expresses himself; he should certainly avoid becoming so conscious of his grammar (or lack of it) that he holds a *post mortem* on each sentence he writes. If his firm employs a secretary or shorthand-typist, who can be relied upon to maintain the essentials of grammar, much can be left to her judgment. There are also numerous books of reference which are helpful, for example: Fowler's *A.B.C. of English Usage, Modern English Usage, The King's English,* Roget's *Thesaurus,* and Eric Partridge's *Usage and Abusage.* There is also our publication *The Right Way to Improve Your English,* paperback, which should be most helpful.

The businessman should remember that his letters will not

be carefully analysed and scrutinized by his correspondents – who, in any event, may be no better grammarians than he – *but they must be easily understood and they must not be ambiguous.*

When you are not quite sure whether a sentence is correctly written, it is a good plan to parse or split it into its component parts. This often exposes mistakes which you may otherwise miss. Take the following sentence: *Just as whisky serves a useful purpose, so should wine, but all too often neither do.* Can you see anything wrong with that sentence? Write it out in full: Just as whisky serves a useful purpose, so should wine serve a useful purpose, but all too often neither the one nor the other *does.* It then becomes apparent where your mistake lies. Errors of case are all too frequent and they often pass unnoticed. You might reply to the question: "To whom does your business belong?" with the words: *To my partner, Mr. Smith, and I.* But you would not say, *To I.* If, therefore, you implement your answer with the one word *to*, you can see your mistake immediately and will change the case of your pronoun, *I,* to the objective, *me.* In everyday speech, you will often hear the phrase, "Between you and I", but you will realise that, in your writing, you should use the grammatically accurate form, *Between you and (between) me.*

SPLIT INFINITIVES

Some years ago, English teachers were putting us through our paces on the question of split infinitives, but recently their dogmatic assertions have been hotly disputed by experts. What *is* a split infinitive? It is an adverb or adverbial phrase inserted between the preposition *to* and the verb of the infinitive. For example: *To quickly walk; to boldly go where no man has gone before. To fully appreciate* is a split infinitive, but *to be fully appreciated* is not. That eminent authority on the correct use of the English language, H. W. Fowler, has summed up the position by saying that it is never advisable to split an infinitive with a long phrase and only to do so when ambiguity or awkwardness would otherwise arise. This gives reasonable scope to most writers.

Length of Sentences

As to the length of his sentences, a wise motto for the beginner might be "Keep them short until you have sufficient command of the English language to lengthen them without sacrificing clarity". Most difficulties only arise when one tries to write sentences beyond one's grasp; one then gets lost in a tangle of confused thought and loose construction. Think out what you want to write before putting it down.

Punctuation

Punctuation has become a matter largely of individual taste, although there are certain fundamental points to remember. As with most subjects, the correct use of punctuation is a great bone of contention among experts. There are two extreme schools of thought – those who favour the academically correct and frequent use of punctuation, and those who insist upon the minimum. The rest of the world falls between these two extremes.

THE FULL STOP

The first, most important and final mark is the full stop. If we say it can safely be used to divide sentences, or sentences and subordinate clauses, which are not closely related to one another, we shall not go far wrong. Too many full stops detract from the flow and rhythm of one's writing and produce a staccato effect, as does also an excess of exclamation marks(!).

The Oxford Concise Dictionary defines a sentence as "A set of words complete in itself, containing subject and predicate and conveying a statement, *question* or *command*,"; (my italics). Sentences can either be *simple* (that is, with a single subject and predicate), *compound* (with more than one of either or both the above), or *complex* (with subordinate clauses).

THE SEMI-COLON

The grouping of several complete sentences which are *closely related in sense* can be divided by semi-colons and this generally makes for easier and more restful reading than the substitution of full stops. It also avoids the use of too many "ands" – a conjunction should not normally follow a semi-colon. For instance: "The remarks you made in your last letter can be more fully discussed at our next meeting; I shall not go further into the matter now.", shows the use of the semi-colon. These two sentences could have been divided by a full stop, but the semi-colon carries less finality and the flow of meaning is maintained without too great a break.

THE COLON

The colon can be used before a quotation – for example: "In his reply, Mr. Jones said: 'I am grateful to our chairman for having summed up the whole matter so simply and expertly'." (A comma could be used in the place of a colon, where the sense is preserved.) Generally the colon can be regarded as meaning "as follows"; it is frequently used to introduce a list.

THE COMMA

A comma provides the shortest break of all. As a rule it should be inserted between adjectives preceding and qualifying substantives – for instance: "An upright, haughty figure" – but not in cases where the last adjective is in closer relation to the substantive than to the preceding adjectives – for instance: "A famous foreign diplomat". It is also used to enclose interpolations, etc., in this way taking the place of parenthesis (or brackets); in these cases the sentence should read quite well *without* the word or words between commas. It should strictly not be used where *and* joins two single words or phrases.

THE APOSTROPHE

The apostrophe, that is, the possessive inverted comma, is simply an abbreviation; thus, "The boy's pencil" is a shortened form meaning "The pencil of the boy". In the plural, the apostrophe follows the "s": "All boy*s*' coats". Note that the abbreviation is *not* used for inanimate objects; one never says "The table's leg" for "The leg of the table". Actually, the apostrophe indicates a missing letter or letters and is also used in such words as "aren't" to show that the "o" of "not" has been omitted. Be careful that it does, in fact, show the position of the missing letter – not "are'nt", as is sometimes seen. As a matter of interest in this connection, the phrase "The boy's pencil" really stands for "The boy his pencil", the "hi" being replaced by an apostrophe to make it less clumsy.

An emerging practice, roundly to be deplored, is the use of what I would term the "intrusive" apostrophe. This mis-use is seen where an apostrophe is inserted into an ordinary plural word. Once limited to greengrocers' signs (banana's, avocado's, etc.) it is now spreading to other shops (video's – two for the price of one) and is even seen in newspaper advertisements (two secretary's needed) (!). The commonest pitfall is in the word *its* (as in for its own sake), often mis-spelt *it's*. But *it's* is short for *it is* (as in *it's a knockout*).

A final warning: in writing, the apostrophe should only be used in the possessive case, it creates a bad impression to use it for lazy abbreviations such as "aren't" and "didn't", except in personal letters. Normally, use "did not" etc.

EXCLAMATION MARKS

There should be no difficulty over the use of question and

exclamation marks, provided you do not confuse the two. Be careful to make sure that your question *is* a question and not a statement of fact or opinion. For instance: "Can you arrange to meet me at 5.30 p.m. on Tuesday next?" is correct, but "I wonder if I could see the manager" can be written without a question mark. An exclamation mark follows an interjection – Alas! Hello!, etc.; it often underlines sarcasm, for example: "I like the English weather!" When following a quotation, as a *comment* by the person quoting, it should be outside the inverted commas, thus: He said "All men are liars"! In such a case it indicates disagreement with the quotation.

DASHES AND BRACKETS

There remains the question of dashes and brackets. In business correspondence they may be seldom necessary, and should be avoided wherever possible unless the writer is confident that he will use them correctly. For example: "Thank you for your letter – and what a nice letter it is!"; "I have enclosed a cheque for £200 (two hundred pounds)." Dashes and brackets are often used for similar purposes, such as clarification, explanation, etc., when it is felt they will make easier reading than with commas. Examples:- "The books, new and old, were on the table", or "The books (new and old) were on the table" or "The books – new and old – were on the table". It will be seen that in this example, commas, brackets and dashes all serve the same purpose.

INVERTED COMMAS, OR "QUOTES"

These are, of course, quotation marks; this gives the clue to their use. An extract from a speech, from what someone has said or written, is put in inverted commas. They are used also to point a metaphor, thus: "Life's fitful fever". They are often found misused in addresses when enclosing the name of a house; the rule to be observed is simple and obvious: Use them when the name is a *quotation*, thus, "Clovelly", but not "Cobblestones".

THE HYPHEN

The hyphen is self-explanatory; common sense will help you to use it correctly. More and more, today, it is being omitted from common words, as for example "book-seller" is more often written "bookseller" (this form has a foreign flavour), or "book seller". The first is strictly correct; the latter rarely seen.

PARAGRAPHS

Paragraphing is not so much a matter of personal taste as to divide a letter into subjects or definite parts of subjects. It is advisable to keep paragraphs reasonably short, if possible; one of more than fifteen lines becomes rather tedious to the reader, who is subconsciously, if not consciously, looking for a break in the continuous flow of text. Do not begin a fresh paragraph, however, to obey this maxim at the expense of continuity but wait until there is a suitable break in the subject matter. Sometimes a short paragraph is used for emphasis and it may (though normally it should not) consist of only one sentence. Do not, therefore, overdo this striving for effect or you may defeat your intention.

Superlatives

The use of double superlatives for emphasis should be avoided. Sufficient emphasis can be obtained with such words as "very"; for example, "great big" is better as "very big" or "very large". "Great" and "big" have the same meaning, therefore "great big" is like saying "big big" – the kind of expression used by children or foreigners only slightly acquainted with the English language. Often, also, the "very" is unnecessary if another word can be used; in our example, "enormous" might do. It's often more effective.

This chapter is the briefest of introductions to the immense subject of grammar and punctuation, and for those who may wish to pursue the matter further – they will obtain much benefit from doing so – there are many books of instruction, both elementary and advanced, and also Adult Education classes.

The businessman must at all costs avoid writing a jumbled and illiterate letter which, apart from the general undesirability of bad writing, may have serious business consequences. Equally, however, he should not spend valuable time pondering over the use (or misuse) of a comma. As the Sabbath was made for man, so is grammar designed for his use. Punctuation cannot make an illiterate letter literate, but it avoids ambiguity and clarifies the meaning which the construction of the sentences might not give without it.

It is the recording of *your* thoughts into well chosen meaningful words with their harmonious flow (which you can check by reading aloud) rather than school teacher's grammar, which gives a letter power, impact and greatness.

3

STYLE AND CONSTRUCTION

Style

Some business people believe that style is essentially the concern of the literateur and that others are, mercifully, not involved. There is no need for me to enter into any academic diatribe on the subject, but I must emphasise that style makes a great difference to the effect of your letter – and there is no short cut to acquiring the ability to express yourself well. It requires continual practice to make your sentences and paragraphs flow smoothly. When you read them aloud, notice whether they *sound* satisfactory. Following this hard road you will enormously improve your writing by reading and absorbing the works of such prose masters as Emerson, Burke, and, to come a little more up-to-date, Winston Churchill, who was acknowledged to be one of our finest writers.

You will also find it generally helpful to study the "leaders" in many of the national dailies and the contribution of any journalists noted for their clarity. Many of the letters to the editor, too, are works of considerable art.

Do not worry too much about style in your everyday writing. Although it will undoubtedly improve a letter, it cannot *make* it; only the ingredients can do that. Remember that what you say matters more than how you say it.

The main function of style, grammar and construction must be to make your writing clear and to convey all you wish to say in as few words as possible. Avoid the impression of "heaviness" in your writing at all costs; sometimes the finest writers are intentionally heavy, but it does not improve an ordinary letter – in fact it will have the opposite effect.

Construction

There are many different ways of setting out a letter. In Government offices and Service departments, paragraphs are often numbered to facilitate easy reference. This is in some ways a good idea because it tends to focus the attention of the letter writer on what he is saying and isolates one theme or development of a theme from the next. It is for this reason preferable to separate headings as there may be more than one paragraph under each head.

The disadvantage of this method is its formality and heaviness. There is an alternative, which is particularly suitable when replying to several letters received from one correspondent on the same day. This is to write the letter under successive headings which should be underlined. You may begin your letter by acknowledging all the letters involved, then proceed to the appropriate headings provided by the material.

Numbered headings, or a combination of both these methods, are excellent for long letters dealing with many subjects as they facilitate reply and quick reference.

With shorter letters it is often necessary to use numbered paragraphs or cross headings, but ensure that new paragraphs are made as new subjects are dealt with, or more frequently as necessary.

Finally, try to get your letter into correct order and if one subject can be made to lead into another, so much the better. In the short letter, where only one or two matters may be dealt with, it is very often a good idea to give a *résumé* in the last line or two, as it holds the recipient's attention to what has already been said. For example:-

ELLIOT RIGHT WAY BOOKS
Kingswood Buildings, Lower Kingswood,
Tadworth, Surrey, KT20 6TD, U.K.

2 February 19XX

Mr John Lawson
Turnkey
Saltford
Somerset
TA1 7XX

Dear Mr Lawson

We have now completed the editorial work on the text of your book and I enclose photocopies of all the pages where we have made alterations. I would be grateful if you could read these and let me know whether these minor changes are acceptable.

I also enclose photocopies of some rough illustrations that our cover artist has sketched. Please may we have your opinion on these as well. Within the next week or two, our artist should have completed the line drawings that are to illustrate your text. As soon as he has done so, I will send you photocopies of them all for your approval.

We have tentatively fixed the publication date for 1 September and need to know if this conflicts with any holiday arrangements you might have made.

I look forward to hearing from you soon with regard to the text alterations, cover design and publication date.

Yours sincerely

The last paragraph sums up all the main points of the letter, focusing attention upon them for the benefit of sender and receiver.

The following example of a muddled sales letter will give the reader some idea of the effect it can have; it provides unlimited scope for misunderstandings:

JONES & HARRIS LIMITED
1 South Parade
Croydon, Surrey, CR1 1XX

12 February 19XX

Mr John Smith
3 High Street
Mogador
Surrey
KT1 2TZ

Dear Mr Smith

I am writing to give you particulars of some 5-drawer filing cabinets which we can offer you at £xxx until the end of the month. I hope you will decide to send a prompt order as these cabinets are selling rapidly and I can guarantee that they are fireproof. As the cost of steel is rising you should gain much by buying at this year's price.

We can also supply five dozen hanging files for £www each, which should be sufficient to fill all the drawers amply, and 10 boxes of steel prong fasteners at a special discount price of £yyy all delivered to your premises.

Your order will receive my prompt attention.

Yours sincerely

The same letter reconstructed:-

Dear Mr Smith

I am writing to make you a special offer of the following:-

1 5-drawer filing cabinet @ £xxx
5 dozen hanging files @ £www
10 boxes steel prong fasteners @ £yyy.

Total cost £zzz, delivered to your premises.* The cabinet is fireproof and is fitted with a safety lock. It is painted in metallic green and there is an A-Z Index for quick referencing.

If you are able to place an order, I shall give it my prompt attention.

Yours sincerely

(*or if you do not wish to emphasise the grand total, replace this sentence with: "All delivered to your premises.")

Reference
When correspondence is large, a simple reference system may be required. Many forms are used, the most common being that in which the initials of the originator and the typist are shown, thus, AGE/MO. Others quote file numbers, contract

numbers, etc. A long and supposedly imposing reference is nonsense unless all of it has a definite purpose for rapid filing and ease of tracing. One drawback of a long and involved reference is that few correspondents seem able to quote correctly more than four figures or letters at one time, and the objects of the reference are defeated. As a matter of courtesy and helpfulness, always quote a correspondent's reference.

Numbering Letters

Where several letters are sent from the same firm to the same recipient in one day, as in large concerns, a policy of numbering letters may be required to facilitate reference.

Setting-out

Most letters (except those 'to the Editor') are typed in single spacing. For short letters, use smaller sheets (e.g. A5 paper) or use a larger type size and pitch. A letter should not be cramped into a small portion of the page. Conversely, do not spread into two pages when one will do. Also, do not use the reverse of the page. If using plain paper for continuation sheets, leave four blank lines at the top of the paper, then at the left-hand margin type the number '2' to indicate this is the second page of the letter. On the line below this (still at the left) type the date, and on the next line type the name of your correspondent. Leave another three or four blank lines before continuing the body of the letter.

It is most important that every letter you write is dated. The date should appear near the top of the page, either at the left- or right-hand margin, depending on your chosen style. Always type the date in full, i.e. 2 September 1989. This avoids confusion, especially when writing to overseas correspondents who often put the month first when abbreviating the date; for example, to abbreviate 2 September 1989 they (in particular in America) would write 9/2/89, while we would write 2/9/89. Therefore the only way to obviate any problems is to write the date in full.

The simplest way to set out a business letter (and that which is recommended here) is to block everything at the left-hand margin. If a reference is included, this can be typed at the left either above or below the date, depending on personal preference, but make sure there is at least one blank line between the reference and the date.

Then, again leaving at least one blank line, type the name and address of your correspondent. Below this, leave at least another blank line and type the salutation. The main body of the letter will begin after another blank line, with blank lines being left between paragraphs. At the end of the letter leave one blank line, then type 'Yours faithfully' (if you addressed your correspondent as 'Dear Sir' or 'Dear Madam') or 'Yours sincerely' (if you addressed your correspondent by name). Your company name then follows typed in capitals on the line directly below this. Leave about five blank lines for your signature and type your name, and on the line below that, your position in the firm, such as Director, Manager, etc. If the letter is to contain any enclosures, type 'Enc' or 'Encs' a few lines below this which will remind you to include the relevant papers.

Equal margins either side add to general appearance; nothing looks worse than an uneven, straggling right-hand margin. Remember the importance of first impressions; a neatly laid-out letter gives an impression of efficiency which may have a good effect on the recipient. Similarly, neatness of typing creates a good impression; a letter spattered with alterations gives the reader a feeling he is dealing with someone who is careless and casual. It is better to re-type correctly than to send it out in this state, although for less important letters an odd alteration is permissible.

Signatures should be written in blue or black ink in preference to more startling colours. The latter may be used to stimulate interest, but unfortunately, they sometimes have the reverse effect.

Here is an example of a letter set out in the style

recommended above.

BLACK & WHITE LIMITED
1 The Square,
Epsom, Surrey, KT1 1XX

Our Ref: ACE/JM

22 February 19XX

The Red River Company Limited
22 Oakehampton Street
Hull
North Humberside
HU11 5ZZ

Dear Sirs

The answer to your letter of 22 January 19XX is that your doors and windows will be delivered to you in the early afternoon of Monday 29 May 19XX.

We assure you we will have someone there to unload them.

With best wishes.

Yours faithfully
BLACK & WHITE LIMITED

....
John Smith
Director

Signed in Absence

A director or partner, or anyone for that matter, may dictate a letter and then have to leave the office before it is typed. In that case, his secretary (if he has confidence in her) or a colleague could add the word "for" or the initials "pp" (meaning "per pro" in Latin) beside the sender's name and sign it on his behalf. Alternatively, the following could be typed instead of the sender's name: "Dictated by Mr A B Black and signed in his absence".

4

FORMS OF ADDRESS AND SUBSCRIPTION

Salutation and Complimentary Closing of Letters

The opening of a letter and its closing remarks remain a matter of personal taste, *within certain well-defined limits.* All I shall do here is to give some guides and suggestions.

Thirty years ago, most letters passing between large companies began: "Dear Sirs" and ended "Yours faithfully", but over recent years a more personal and friendly note has been introduced. Today, the director of one company will write to the director of another company in quite friendly terms, and the "Dear Sirs" and "Yours faithfully" will be discarded. Instead, he will either write "Dear Mr Smith" or even "Dear John".

On the whole, the rule is that if you don't know the name of the particular individual to whom you are writing, address him as "Dear Sir" or "Dear Madam", as appropriate. But if you are answering a letter you have received, reply to the person who signed the letter, e.g. "Dear Mr Jones", or "Dear Mrs Smith". After some correspondence (including perhaps telephone conversations and personal meetings) you may progress to being on Christian name terms with your correspondent.

"Yours faithfully" is the accepted business ending to a letter which begins "Dear Sir(s)" or "Dear Madam"; while

"Yours sincerely" is the ending for a letter beginning "Dear Mr Smith" or "Dear John".

One word of warning: business correspondents should avoid becoming too familiar during early acquaintanceship in case the need should ever arise for rather strongly-worded correspondence to pass from one to the other. If, therefore, you have been in the habit of writing *My dear Jack*, and then find yourself in the position of having to dispatch a *Dear Sir, Unless . . .*, you will be in a rather awkward situation. Where your correspondent has attempted to take advantage of your friendly relationship, you may have to revert to the more formal *Dear Sir*, and in certain extreme cases, merely the word *Sir*.

I would just like to say a word here about one practice which is indulged in and which, although time-consuming, is attractive. It would only be used in an important letter and the idea of it is to convey the extra special personal touch.

The body of the letter is typed in the ordinary way but your secretary leaves the opening line and the closing line blank. You (the writer of the letter) then fill in *in ink* "Dear John" or "Dear Mr Black" or "Dear Sir William" as the case may be and at the end "Yours sincerely", again *in ink*. This tends to lift the letter out of the ordinary.

Addressing Envelopes

Unless the contents of your letters are strictly personal or confidential, it is not wise to mark your envelope accordingly. Your correspondent may be away when your letter arrives, and your "personal" address may prevent the opening of the envelope by his or her deputy.

It is customary to add the words *Messrs* before all firms trading by name – for example, Messrs A G Blank & Tomson, but not before companies or firms trading under impersonal titles, for example, The Cloud Formation Company Limited. One should not really abbreviate the names of addressees; for instance, if the firm is Messrs Alfred Canford Johnson & Company, it is safer not to write to them as Messrs A C Johnson & Company, or your letter may be delivered to the wrong firm.

For individuals, if male, "Mr" followed by the name is used, unless there is any other title. Formerly, "Esq" was used for men who owned land, and "Mr" was only used where someone was in a minor position or a very small way of trade; nowadays, as class distinctions have become less obvious, "Mr" has been adopted as the general rule. "Mr" can also be used when the person's initials are unknown, but in this case, when writing to an individual in a firm, it is more polite to send the letter addressed to the firm, marked for attention, thus:

FIELD & FIELD LIMITED
253 High Street, Lincoln, LN1 7YY

2 November 19XX

For the attention of Mr Binks

Smith & Smith Limited
21 North Road
Epsom
Surrey
KT1 5TT

Dear Sirs

If you are writing to a woman and you know her marital status, then address her as 'Miss' or 'Mrs' accordingly. But if you don't know whether she is married or not, or if you know she prefers the title 'Ms', use that instead.

On envelopes the commonest error is to place the name and address too high, where the postmark interferes with it; it should be confined, as far as possible, to the lower half.

Insufficiently addressed envelopes are the cause of much irritation and delay; all addresses should be carefully checked and complete – in Great Britain, as in many other countries, people have been allocated Post Codes. These should be printed at the end of your address on your notepaper, and you should put them on the envelope of any addressee who has one, to speed delivery.

A letter is incompletely addressed if the post code is given without the town to which it refers. In the case of any but the very largest cities or county towns, the county is necessary too, e.g.

The Door Company
588 Old Street
LEATHERHEAD
Surrey
KT24 5LQ

The Door Company
101 Prince of Wales Road
NORWICH
NR1 1JJ

The name and address of the recipient of the letter is included on the letter itself (at the top left-hand corner immediately above the salutation) in case the envelope becomes defaced; if a copy is taken of the letter, the address will help the typist or filing clerk to see at a glance to which file it belongs if no other reference system is used. It is sometimes the custom, in more personal letters, to place the recipient's name and address at the bottom left-hand corner.

Forms of Address

Untitled People

MAN	Dear Sir or Dear Mr (Mr on envelope)
WOMAN	Dear Madam or Dear Mrs or Dear Miss or Dear Ms (Mrs, Miss or Ms on envelope)
TWO OR MORE MARRIED WOMEN	Mesdames
TWO OR MORE SPINSTERS	The Misses
Two business women can be addressed simply in the salutation of a letter as	Ladies
HUSBAND AND WIFE	Mr and Mrs (No initials of degrees, etc.)
BOYS UNDER 14	Master

Persons of Rank

DUKE	His Grace the Duke of	My Lord Duke or Your Grace (Refer to as "Your Grace") (I remain, my Lord Duke)
DUCHESS	Her Grace the Duchess of	Madam ("Your Grace") (I remain, Madam)
MARQUESS	The Most Hon. the Marquess of	My Lord Marquess ("Your Lordship") (I remain, my Lord Marquess)
MARCHIONESS	The Most Hon. the Marchioness of	Madam ("Your Ladyship") (I remain, Madam)

EARL	The Right Hon. the Earl of	My Lord ("Your Lordship") (I remain, my Lord)
COUNTESS	The Right Hon. the Countess of	Madam ("Your Ladyship") (I remain, Madam)
VISCOUNT	The Right Hon. the (Lord) Viscount	My Lord ("Your Lordship") (I remain, my Lord)
VISCOUNTESS	The Right Hon. the Viscountess, or, The Viscountess	Madam ("Your Ladyship") (I remain, Madam)
BARON	The Right Hon. Lord, or, The Lord	My Lord ("Your Lordship") (I remain, my Lord)
BARONESS	The Right Hon. the, or, The Baroness	My Lady ("Your Ladyship") (I remain, my Lady)
BARONET	Sir James Milwall Bart. or Bt.	Sir (I am, Sir)
BARONET'S WIFE	Lady Milwall	Madam ("Your Ladyship") (I am, Madam)
KNIGHT	Sir John Newell	Sir (between friends, Dear Sir John) (I am, Sir)
KNIGHT'S WIFE	Lady Newell	Madam (between friends, Dear Lady XX) (I am, Madam)
ARCHBISHOP (English)	His Grace the Lord Archbishop of	My Lord Archbishop ("Your Grace")
BISHOP	The Right Rev. the Lord Bishop of, or, The Lord Bishop of	My Lord Bishop ("Your Lordship")

DEAN	The Very Rev. the Dean of	Very Rev. Sir (formal); Mr Dean
CLERGY	The Rev. William Lockwood (if a Doctor of Divinity, add DD)	Rev. Sir (formal); Dear Sir, Dear Mr, or, if a DD, Dear Dr
JUDGE	The Hon. Mr Justice	Sir
PRIVY COUNCILLORS	The Right Hon. Michael Quarterly MP	Sir (Yours faithfully)
MEMBERS OF PARLIAMENT	Mr David Jones MP Sir Roy Farjeon MP	Sir or Dear Sir (Yours faithfully)
DOCTOR	Dr Peter Ransome	Dear Sir, or, Dear Dr
SURGEON	Mr Philip Palmer FRCS	Dear Sir, or, Dear Mr

Commissioned officers of HM Forces are addressed by rank, together with decorations, if any. Naval officers, add RN. Army officers may have their arm of Service added, e.g. RA, RE.

5

THE RISKS OF LETTER WRITING

Libel and Defamation of Character

Libel and defamation of character are, of course, two very serious risks, but there are many others – of which the giving of offence (whether intentional or not) must have a high place.

Care must also be taken, when describing goods, not to contravene the Trade Descriptions Act.

The copyright of a letter belongs to the writer of it; if A writes you a letter, you are not entitled to take extracts from it to pass on to B or with a view to any form of publication or publicity without A's permission. If A had made libellous or defamatory remarks in his letter, you would be extremely unwise to pass them on and might find yourself in legal trouble.

The libel position is hedged about with so many technicalities that only an expert can give an opinion on any particular case – and even the opinion of an expert might be proved wrong in a Court of Law. On the other hand, a great deal of privilege is allowed, provided precautions are taken. Equally, custom and some knowledge of the person to whom you are writing play their parts in such matters. One sensible precaution is that the originator should himself put any important letter into its envelope, after reading and signing it, to ensure that no mistakes are made.

In the ordinary course of business many situations arise which call for strong wording; I give below some examples of letters which are perfectly "safe", provided the letter is addressed personally to a director or senior official of the firm concerned and that the words "Private and Confidential" appear on the envelope and directly above the recipient's name on the letter itself. Always remember, however, that if in any doubt, be *very careful* what you write.

Imagine, for example, that I have bought one hundred leather wallets from a representative. On delivery, I discover they are not leather but are made of imitation skin. I have nothing in writing, but wish to get the correct position established at the earliest moment.

PARKER & PARKER
16 Fore Street
Bury, Lancashire, BL2 5TT

5 April 19XX

PRIVATE AND CONFIDENTIAL
Mr W J Baxter
Managing Director
Baxter & Johnson Limited
Market Square
Gorton
Manchester
M41 4EJ

Dear Sir

A week ago your representative called

here and sold me one hundred leather wallets at £20 each. On delivery, I found that these wallets are made of some imitation skin, and I am accordingly writing to inform you I cannot accept these at the price you charge, i.e., £20 each. In my view, a reasonable price for these imitation leather articles would be £5 each, and if you are not prepared to reduce them accordingly I propose to return the consignment.

I await your reply.

Yours faithfully
PARKER & PARKER

D E PARKER

This letter contains an implicit accusation, but there is nothing dangerous about it as it is addressed personally to the head of the firm concerned, who should open it so that it cannot get into the hands of any other members of the staff – an eventuality which might affect the situation.

I give below a second example:

SMITH & JONES LIMITED
241 Fanshaw Street
Lincoln, LN2 5ZZ

10 June 19XX

PRIVATE AND CONFIDENTIAL

Mr J P Fullsome
Fullsome & Harding Limited
301 Church End
Bedford
MK2 5HH

Dear Sir

I have just heard you are offering our 5cm oak planks, bearing our brand, as being two years dry. If you will refer to our quotation and confirmation of order, you will find that the planks were sold to you as one year dry.

This letter is to request you to alter your offers to conform with the terms under which the goods were sold, as we cannot allow our brand to be misrepresented.

An acknowledgement of this letter, and your agreement to the suggested course of action, will be appreciated.

Yours faithfully
SMITH & JONES LIMITED

G H Smith
Director

The following letters constitute correspondence between Blandish & Owen Limited and the Writa Pen Company Limited:

BLANDISH & OWN LIMITED
The Pen Shop
Church Street, Anytown, AA1 3ZZ

2 July 19XX

PRIVATE AND CONFIDENTIAL
Mr G Stanford Brown
Sales Manager
The Writa Pen Company Limited
Broad Street
Birmingham
B2 6UU

Dear Sir

A very serious matter has arisen in

connection with the delivery of 1,000 fountain pens against our order number 0783.

We regret to inform you that these pens have proved extremely unsatisfactory. Frequent complaints have been received from customers to the effect that the pens leak and will not write without blotting. Quite frankly, they fall considerably below our usual standard and we think the best way out of the difficulty will be for you to authorise the return of the balance of the consignment, which is 937 pens.

The functioning of the pens has been compared with the sample left by your representative, and in our view the bulk of the shipment contains defects and is inferior to the sample.

Your comments will be appreciated.

Yours faithfully
BLANDISH & OWEN LIMITED

K C Blandish

THE WRITA PEN COMPANY LIMITED
Broad Street, Birmingham, B2 6UU

4 July 19XX

Mr K C Blandish
Blandish & Owen Limited
The Pen Shop
Church Street
Anytown
AA1 3ZZ

Dear Sir

In reply to your letter of 2 July 19XX, we would point out that all our pens are manufactured to be, and to the best of our knowledge are, identical in design and performance. In any case, as you have accepted delivery and broken bulk, we cannot accept the return of the goods or entertain any claim.

Yours faithfully
THE WRITA PEN COMPANY LIMITED

G Stanford Brown
Sales Manager

BLANDISH & OWEN LIMITED
The Pen Shop
Church Street, Anytown, AA1 3ZZ

7 July 19XX

PRIVATE AND CONFIDENTIAL
Mr G Stanford Brown
Sales Manager
The Writa Pen Company Limited
Broad Street
Birmingham
B2 6UU

Dear Sir

We are surprised at the attitude adopted in your letter of 4 July 19XX. In view of the fact that the pens are manufactured articles we do not believe that bulk being broken has any bearing on the case as the flaws were not visible. Before taking further action, do you not think it would be wise to send a representative to inspect the goods?

Yours faithfully
BLANDISH & OWEN LIMITED

K C Blandish

A dangerous reply would be one which inferred that you intended telling the whole trade of the treatment received from the Writa Pen Company. That might provoke legal action for malicious defamation of character. Although the firm had admittedly behaved badly, they might be legally within their rights. On the other hand, it is customary to warn your friends against trading with such a concern, provided the warning is given verbally to people upon whose discretion you can depend.

Should the firm in question be a member of any trade association, it is often worthwhile to advise them you intend to put the matter before their association unless they adopt a more reasonable attitude; many firms will be prepared to reach some amicable agreement rather than jeopardise their reputation. It *rarely* pays to go to law, but in certain instances it is wise to get a solicitor's opinion and consider it.

Among other matters that may arise are letters with insurance companies, where you have a genuine complaint. Let us imagine that the insurance company, after negotiation, has declined to pay you £xxxx for damages to which you feel entitled, and that their offer has been £xxx. A suitable reply is given overleaf:

JOHN SMITH
17 Devonshire Street
London, SW13 9JG

21 October 19XX

The Barter Insurance Company Limited
Beacon House
Crossgate
Liverpool
L9 3XR

Dear Sirs

With reference to your letter of 17 October 19XX, I cannot accept the £xxx offered, and must insist on the full £xxxx compensation to which I feel entitled. This is the lowest figure I am prepared to accept, and unless this matter is settled to my satisfaction within fourteen days I shall regretfully be obliged to issue a writ.

Yours faithfully

John Smith

This rather strong line will usually achieve results because large companies dislike going to law unless they are sure they have a good case. The same remarks apply to any other similar instances. If you take a strong line you will nearly always win your point, *provided you are in the right.*

A LIBELLOUS LETTER

SMITH & JONES LIMITED

High Street, Anytown, Surrey, KT1 2ZZ

17 October 19XX

Cash & King
44 North Road
London
SW99 6KK

Dear Sirs

Your representative called here yesterday and offered a representative of our firm a £xxx bribe to take no action over the question of the inferior quality of your recent delivery of barrels.

We hereby notify you that we are closing your account and you may inform your representative that he will not be required to come here again; in fact it would be wiser for him not to do so.

Yours faithfully

C Thomas

Even though it may be true that the representative offered some form of bribe, it would obviously be extremely difficult to prove; in putting your accusation in writing you would immediately expose yourself to a very serious risk – defamation of character. The latter part of the letter also contains a hidden threat, and threatening letters are particularly dangerous.

Letters Asking for Payment

Terms for payment vary in different trades, but in them all there will be good payers, slow payers and those who never intend to pay at all. Slow payers must be treated with care. It is an unfortunate human weakness that most of us are gravely offended when asked for money. Many firms have lost accounts which might have developed into good propositions because the accountant, cashier, representative, or even the Managing Director has written a tactless letter regarding some outstanding account.

It is best to treat each customer as an individual, and if an account has been rendered more than once it is customary to add to it the words: "Kindly remit", while if it has been rendered two or three times some stronger request can be made – for example, "As this account is now three months overdue, please remit within seven days".

On the other hand, many firms prefer to include a letter with the account asking for payment. It is wise to take the greatest care in such a matter or much valuable goodwill may be sacrificed. If the letter is worded diplomatically, the recipient is less liable to be offended. Remember always to address your letter to a senior official of the firm concerned and to include the words "Private and Confidential" on both the envelope and the letter.

You could send a letter similar to this one:

MASTERS & CASE LIMITED
Farnborough House
Old Portsmouth
Hampshire, PO5 6XZ

5 June 19XX

PRIVATE AND CONFIDENTIAL
The Manager
Whiteway, James & Tait Limited
Chain Buildings
Ventnor
Isle of Wight
PO3 9LP

Dear Sir

We enclose our account for £550.45, which is now two months overdue. We feel you may have overlooked this, and shall be glad of a remittance as soon as possible.

Yours faithfully

G Case
Manager

If the debtor ignores your request, sterner measures must be taken:

MASTERS & CASE LIMITED
Farnborough House
Old Portsmouth
Hampshire, PO5 6XZ

5 July 19XX

PRIVATE AND CONFIDENTIAL
The Manager
Whiteway, James & Tait Limited
Chain Buildings
Ventnor
Isle of Wight
PO3 9LP

Dear Sir

Your account is now three months overdue and you will appreciate that we cannot run our business unless we receive payment for goods delivered.

We shall be glad if you will make payment by return, or let us have some suggestion as to how and when you will pay so that we may consider it.

Yours faithfully

G Case
Manager

A stronger demand might be worded as follows:

MASTERS & CASE LIMITED
Farnborough House
Old Portsmouth
Hampshire, PO5 6XZ

5 July 19XX

PRIVATE AND CONFIDENTIAL
The Manager
Whiteway, James & Tait Limited
Chain Buildings
Ventnor
Isle of Wight
PO3 9LP

Dear Sir

We are writing to request payment of our account, which has remained overdue for three months.

Unless payment is received within seven days we regret we have no alternative but to issue a writ without further notice.

Yours faithfully

G Case
Manager

The following kind of legal approach can be very successful:

PRIVATE AND CONFIDENTIAL

TO: (Name)
OF: (Address)

SUM DUE: (Amount in words)

BE ADVISED Papers are in preparation for legal proceedings to be taken against you in your nearest Court to recover the sum of £xxx when application will also be made to that Court for an Order to charge the total costs of this Action against you.

IF you wish to avoid such Action by payment of the amount due, urgently send it to this address to arrive not later than (date - allow ten days, making sure it will not occur during a weekend; if so, go on to the Monday).

DATED (Date in words)
SIGNED (Signature)

N.B. This type of letter should be sent by Recorded Delivery.

It is often better not to write but to call in person. Sometimes you might have to accept a part payment in full settlement.

With *dishonest* people, firm handling and the threat of a writ may produce the desired result.

It may have been obvious that I have avoided any suggestion of actually putting an unpaid account into the hands of a lawyer. Many people who do not pay accounts are also not deterred by solicitors; they know they can delay any legal action for some weeks by an exchange of correspondence – all of which will cost you money. In fact, in the U.K., it is not worth instructing solicitors to issue a writ unless the amount of money is substantial. For smaller amounts, a debt-collecting company can be used (these generally charge a percentage of money recovered), but this will not often succeed if you have already done everything possible yourself.

Issuing Writs

Do not lightly issue a writ unless you mean it and believe it to be worthwhile. If you do, issue it after having given due notice. The warning, however, will often prove to be sufficient. If you issue the writ instead of employing a legal firm to do it, it will be cheaper and probably just as effective. If you prefer to work through a lawyer, do not allow him to procrastinate unduly; request him to send a short note, which he may insist on doing for the sake of his reputation, requesting payment or threatening a writ. If no reply is received, *instruct* your solicitor to attend to the writ. What you must avoid is to allow the lawyer to send his clerk, write several letters, make phone calls, etc., or you may find that even if he gets the money in the end much of it has been dissipated by his expenses and costs.

6

SIMPLE LETTERS

By simple letters I am referring to letters which deal with comparatively unimportant subjects; this leads to the statement that many letters should never be written at all. Letters are sometimes sent to enclose invoices and statements, cheques, catalogues and so forth. The businessman will do well to remember that a letter costs a lot more than the stamp. There is the time involved, the paper and other materials used; every business should do its best to cut down *superfluous* paperwork. This does not mean, however, that letter writing should be limited to those which are absolutely essential; the question of courtesy and the value of having copies of correspondence must be considered.

For example, a firm may have asked other firms for quotations to supply some stationery, and as a result may have received six quotations. It will not be necessary to acknowledge each quotation. On the other hand, for a shipbuilding firm which has solicited quotations for specifications in steel or timber, possibly running into hundreds of items, it would only be polite to acknowledge the quotations in appreciation of the immense amount of work which will have been done by the estimating departments of the possible suppliers. Such matters are really only questions of common sense.

Copies

In many cases, copies of simple letters are unnecessary and merely a waste of time. In some large concerns, copies of *all* correspondence may be essential, not only for filing purposes but to advise other departments of action already taken. However with small firms and one-man businesses a vast amount of time and paper can be saved by writing on the original letter the word "acknowledged" and the date and any other explanatory remarks necessary.

Copies of all important letters must, however, be retained for future reference, and, of course, they would be required in any legal proceedings. If a typist is employed, the dictator of the letters must, therefore, remember to mention which letters require copies being made.

Example Letters

Here are some examples of simple letters:

COOK & FISHER LIMITED
7-9 Wharfedale Road
London N53 2PP

22 May 19XX

A & B Carstairs Limited
Silvertown Road
Leamington Spa
Warwickshire
CV3 8UI

Dear Sirs

<u>Re: Order No. 9654</u>

In reply to your letter of 20 May 19XX we are pleased to advise you that the goods will be delivered to your warehouse on 15 June 19XX.

Yours faithfully
COOK & FISHER LIMITED

J A Cook
Manager

COURT & KING LIMITED
189 Leadenhall Street
London S1 4HY

14 May 19XX

A B Troutbeck & Company Limited
Fashion Court
Sevenoaks
Kent
TN37 1PP

Dear Sirs

Thank you for your enquiry of 12 May 19XX. We will send you a quotation within a few days.

Yours faithfully
COURT & KING LIMITED

A B Burke
Manager

HOWARD & HOWARD LIMITED
White Buildings, Fenner Lane
London, EC2 6LY

21 September 19XX

Mr Desmond Carter
Fancourt House
Highway Road
Croydon
CR9 1UT

Dear Mr Carter

Mr Smith has asked me to acknowledge your postcard of yesterday's date and to say that we hope to call upon you on Monday next, 25 September 19XX, at 4 p.m.

If this suggested time is inconvenient to you, please telephone to let us know; if we do not hear from you we shall assume our proposed arrangement stands.

Yours sincerely
HOWARD & HOWARD LIMITED

S K French

SUPER BUSINESS MACHINES LIMITED
68 Gordon Street
London, WC1A 2SP

5 August 19XX

Mr R D Crisp
9 George Lane
London
W1R 7BP

Dear Sir

In reply to your enquiry of 2 August 19XX, regarding the price of the Denton-Mullet fax machine, this retails at £xxxx (plus V.A.T.). We would be pleased to give you a demonstration should you care to call on us at our showrooms at the above address.

Yours faithfully
SUPER BUSINESS MACHINES LIMITED

A T Smith
Sales Manager

CASH & CARTWRIGHT LIMITED
Challenge House, Russell Square
London, N15 6UY

2 February 19XX

Mr J L Chalfont
Rokesby
Aylesbury
Buckinghamshire
HP3 6YY

Dear Mr Chalfont

Thank you for your letter of 1 February 19XX.

I am carrying out some research into the question you raise and will write to you again in a few days' time.

Yours sincerely
CASH & CARTWRIGHT LIMITED

A S Newman

CASH & CARTWRIGHT LIMITED
Challenge House, Russell Square
London, N15 6UY

4 February 19XX

Mr J R D Blackburn
Fencings
Fallowfield
Lancashire
LA3 9OP

Dear Mr Blackburn

Very many thanks for the telephone message which I received this morning. The information will be extremely useful to our Public Relations Department.

Yours sincerely
CASH & CARTWRIGHT LIMITED

A W C Wittering

As stated at the beginning of this chapter, there is no need to enclose a letter with an invoice, or cheque, etc. This also usually applies when sending small gifts at Christmas, such as calendars or diaries. In most cases, a compliments slip would suffice. There are, however, occasions – especially in dealing with good customers – where Christmas cards or calendars may be sent with personal letters; alternatively, personal letters alone may be preferred. The following is a simple letter which would be appropriate in such an event:

FITZGERALD & SMITH LIMITED
15 Danebury Road
Portsmouth, Hampshire, PO5 7YY

15 December 19XX

Mr W Y Aitcheson
Messrs Deans & Aitcheson
Dryscoll Mount
Farnham
Surrey
GU7 9OP

Dear Mr Aitcheson

I am writing to wish you and all the members of your firm a very happy Christmas and good fortune in the coming year.

The co-operation which you have extended to us during these most difficult times has been greatly appreciated; it is to be hoped that the future will be easier for us all.

With kind regards.

Yours sincerely
FITZGERALD & SMITH LIMITED

James Fitzgerald
Managing Director

It is a general rule never to write letters unless they are necessary; keep simple letters clear, short and courteous.

7

REPLYING TO LETTERS

System in Replying

For each person who writes a poor initial letter, there are ten who write bad replies. It might almost be said that the standard of the initial letters in business today is reasonably high or at least passable, whereas the standard of the replies is appallingly low.

There is no secret about this; large numbers of answers are bad simply because the writers do not follow an organised method of dealing with their correspondence. One satisfactory way of answering a letter is to make pencilled marginal notes of any points which occur to you as you read it quickly through the first time. It can then be re-read more slowly and additional notes made. The reply should be dictated to a secretary or into a tape recorder or typed straight on to your typewriter/word processor (if you do your own typing), or, of course, handwritten, and, as the letter is composed, a pencilled line should be drawn through the original letter, *marking off each paragraph as it is dealt with. When the line passes completely through the text, you can be reasonably sure that no section of the letter has been overlooked.*

Many people – perhaps the majority – deal with two or three points and forget the rest, or they may go off at a tangent and omit to answer several important matters.

Do not forget that every reply costs money. A business friend of mine has computed the amount per letter to be frightening. It is often feasible to include other material in your reply. This point should receive careful attention, because on many occasions answering a letter provides an opportunity for the introduction of some new and possibly profitable subject, or the inclusion of a leaflet of a new product.

From what has been said, it should not be inferred that if you get silly questions asked in your mail, you are obliged to reply to them. There are a few people who write for catalogues, particulars and technical information rather for the fun of the thing and, if encouraged by lengthy and explanatory replies, might end up by absorbing all your time. In such cases, some of the points may have to be ignored and a short reply sent as a matter of courtesy. There are other letters which require no reply at all – and here I include the insulting letter which may occasionally be received. Frequently, the wisest course is to ignore the writer. The man or woman who writes a letter to annoy you does so in the hope of succeeding, but only the things which we allow to hurt us do so, and if the insolent communication is merely filed away or put into the waste paper basket, it does no harm.

If a customer writes to you, requesting urgent information it is hardly necessary to say that it should be supplied at once. What *is* perhaps worth mentioning is that, very often, matters requiring haste can be speeded up by posting early in the day.

It is impossible to deal with every conceivable angle of this question, but one very important rule is that if you are ever behind with your payments and receive a letter requesting a settlement, an immediate reply in explanation should be sent. Many firms regard the ignoring of a letter asking for money overdue as insolence – as indeed it is. If a prompt reply is dispatched with a careful explanation of the difficulties and an indication of a payment date, much trouble may be avoided, sometimes serious trouble.

8

DICTATION AND SECRETARIES

Dictation is a pleasant way of dealing with correspondence and may give a better flow to your style. Some people find dictation difficult, but practice should help. Start with short, easy letters, and as your confidence grows, try dictating longer letters. It would help to make a list of the important points you wish to mention, in the order in which you want to present them. This should avoid omissions. It is boring for a secretary to wait for someone to gather his thoughts together, who then makes stabs at what he wants to say, only to change his mind. Sudden, galloping dictation is just as difficult. Secretaries prefer to work for somebody who dictates fluently and clearly.

A newly-qualified college leaver has learned the theory but has yet to gain the practical experience which a job will give her. She will need time to get used to the routine, and the new people. It is important to try to put her at her ease. She may have to learn some specialised terms which apply to your particular trade or profession, and in the first few weeks she may be rather slow and possibly inaccurate. Dictate steadily, so that she can keep up with you. As her confidence builds up, her skills will improve too. Many secretaries would like the opportunity to use their own initiative. Inexperienced secretaries could start by answering enquiries or dealing with routine letters. Experienced secretaries will be able to answer many letters, and deal with most situations that might arise in their employer's absence. Both will need to learn your particular way of answering correspondence.

Dictating Machines

For letters, there is no substitute for a good secretary. She can remember when you last wrote to Mr Smith, or quickly recap on the dictation when it has been interrupted by a telephone call. The tape or cassette can be rewound, but it takes longer.

However nowadays most companies use dictating machines and have a pool of audio typists sharing the work which has previously been fed into tape recorders.

When dictating for audio typing, you must give all the information *first,* i.e. which type style to use (where applicable), which paper, etc. Any mistakes made during the dictation should be erased from the tape and re-dictated.

Although I feel this is an impersonal method of working, it does have many advantages. A busy person can use a tape recorder whilst travelling to and from work, or on business trips. Also, if a typist is ill, letters can be transcribed at a later date, or by somebody else. In addition, a typist can get on with other work while letters, etc. are being put onto the machine.

Finally, don't forget to thank your secretary when she has done well. Respect her intelligence and so far as possible try to use the full extent of her abilities. This is rarely easy because so much office work (indeed any work) is repetitive and tends to be dull. If she is good, look after her.

It's the art of keeping what, in another area, is called a 'happy ship' that is so important; that's not always easy, although like most things in life, it ought to be.

9

LETTERS FOR SPECIAL OCCASIONS

Letters of Introduction

Many years ago letters of introduction were in fairly common use, but today they are not often called for, except possibly for journeys abroad – when they may be written on behalf of a traveller who is covering fresh territory or to establish identity. Their purpose is to introduce one person or body of persons to another; they should be brief, courteous and to the point. For example:

HUGHES & HUGHES LIMITED
16–32 Whardale Point
Cheapside, London, EC1 7YZ

17 April 19XX

Tempest Agricultural Sundries Company
266 Kenyatta Concourse
Nairobi
Kenya

Dear Sirs

I am writing to introduce Mr John Jackson, our agricultural representative, in the hope that you may be able to offer him some assistance.

Mr Jackson is making a study of crop yields in certain areas of Kenya and I shall be extremely grateful if you are able to give him any information which will help him to carry out his work.

Yours faithfully
HUGHES & HUGHES LIMITED

Simon K Medway

SMITH & JONES LIMITED
Mitre House, Terrence Court,
Bath, Avon, BA1 9TT

3 February 19XX

For the attention of Mr William Paul

Firm Foundations Limited
7-11 Westminster Steps
London
SW9 7UZ

Dear Mr Paul

Mr David Brett, who has been with us for two-and-a-half years as an apprentice draughtsman, is most anxious to enter the building trade, and it occurs to me that you may be able to help him, either by considering his capabilities if you happen to have a suitable vacancy in your own firm, or by advising him as to the best method of obtaining the kind of work for which he is looking.

Needless to say, I shall be very pleased if you can do anything for Mr Brett; during his service with us he has been perfectly satisfactory.

Yours sincerely
SMITH & JONES LIMITED

John Smith

Do not give introductions too freely as there may be repercussions, and be particularly careful if you recommend somebody as being trustworthy; human nature being what it is, there is a danger in assumptions. My remarks under this heading will be reinforced when I deal with the writing of references.

Letters of Application

Job application letters can be difficult as it is not always known to whom one is writing because some advertisements appear under the name of a management consultancy, an employment agency or a box or telephone number.

Not all applications are in reply to advertisements. There is, of course, the method of writing to a particular firm in the line of business which the applicant is anxious to enter. When he knows the person to whom he is writing he can formulate some idea of the *type* of letter likely to appeal; and as individuals differ so much, there is little to be gained by elaboration here.

I must now stress several points in connection with such letters:

Firstly, keep your application as short as is consistent with the information required.

Secondly, study the wording of the advertisement carefully because from it you may be able to judge much about the advertiser. The old-fashioned firm of wine merchants, seeking a representative for the Midlands, will probably be best approached by an impersonal letter, carefully phrased, giving all details asked for and full particulars of your career. On the other hand, the firm looking for a "live-wire" salesman possessing initiative, drive and a forceful personality, could receive an application worded in a lighter and more aggressive vein, though I must add that it is safer to err on the side of dignity than the reverse.

Thirdly, the applicant must read the requirements for the

post closely and in his reply must state clearly which he is able to fulfil. He must also ensure that he has answered the advertisement *fully*; for instance, if he is asked to state the salary required he should do so and not evade the question.

Perhaps the most important factor in an application is the *tone* of the letter, and in general the applicant is well advised to show keenness for the post. One reason for keeping your application short is that if you give too many particulars, you may thereby jeopardise your chances of an interview.

An example letter which might reasonably stand some chance of success is given opposite:

ADVERTISEMENT:
Old-established London publishing firm, with long list of successful works of fiction, requires sales representative to cover Scotland, Northern Ireland and the North of England. Must live in Glasgow. Reply stating experience, age and salary required. Box No. 31158.

REPLY

39 Platton Terrace
Glasgow, G79 9QQ

12 August 19XX

Box No. 31158

Please treat in strict confidence

Dear Sirs

In answer to your advertisement in today's issue of the Glasgow Herald, I give below the particulars requested.

1. I am at present employed with Plowden & Monck Limited, of London, having been with them for three years as their representative covering the territories you mention in your advertisement. My only reason for wishing to make a change is that I may improve my position. Prior to my present work, I learned the business with Atkinson & Finlay Limited and was with them for seven years, during the last three of which I was Sales Representative in the Midlands.

2. Age: 36.

3. I am asking a salary of £xxxxx per annum, but if it is your wish to pay on a salary plus commission basis, I should be pleased to discuss the matter with you.

4. May I stress that I am particularly interested in the fiction market and have considerable experience of it. I know the buyers well in the areas I have covered, and I find that being a Scotsman is a great advantage in the North.

I hope that I may be granted an interview.

Yours faithfully

John Smith

Apart from answering advertisements, there are other methods of obtaining jobs. As already explained, writing to a firm that conducts business in which you are particularly interested sometimes brings satisfactory results. It is, of course, a "hit or miss" method, but there is always the chance that your application may coincide with a decision to increase staff, or there may be a vacancy to fill. An appropriate letter is given below:

Tanfield
Burnham Road
Liverpool, L6 9LJ

20 May 19XX

The Personnel Officer
The Wilson, Heffer Timber Co. Ltd.
The Pines
56 South Street
Birkenhead
Merseyside
L78 9IK

Dear Sir or Madam

I write to enquire if you have an opening for a sales representative.

I was educated at the King's School, Chester, leaving at 17, and have since been employed by Edward J Kellett & Company Limited, of Manchester, until a week ago, when the firm closed down. I worked in their Order and Accounts Department, and am therefore accustomed to trade terms, calculations and market trends. I have also a fairly extensive knowledge of the different kinds of timber.

I am most anxious to become a sales

representative because I have a keen interest in timber and its uses, am fond of travelling and able to make contacts easily.

I enclose a copy of my curriculum vitae which gives further information.

If you have a suitable vacancy on your staff, I should be grateful if you would grant me an interview.

Yours faithfully

John Jones

References or Testimonials

The composition of a testimonial calls for knowledge and care. This fixed rule should be observed: never write a testimonial unless the person for whom it is written has been known to you for a considerable time, and you possess a good deal of information about him. One is apt to write testimonials out of kindness, but remember that what you say may carry considerable weight and may influence some extremely important decision. The result may be far from kindness to someone!

Some years ago, a friend of mine, a leading figure in his industry, was asked by a life-long friend to write a reference for the latter's son. Apart from an occasional meeting, this young man was unknown to him, but in view of the long friendship between the boy's father and himself, he willingly agreed to write a letter of introduction somewhat on the following lines:

Fansham House
Chagford
Devon, TQ4 8LK

5 August 19XX

This letter is to introduce Mr Roy X; I hope you will be able to do something to help him to obtain satisfactory work. He is a hard-working, honest and energetic young man.

The statement on his capabilities and character was simply repeated from what his father had said. On the strength of this introduction, the young man obtained an important post in a large concern and everything appeared to be satisfactory. About two years later, however, my friend received a letter from one of the directors of the company informing him that Mr X had embezzled a large sum of money and had subsequently disappeared, taking with him a lot of property belonging to the firm. I quote this unfortunate incident as an illustration of the pitfalls into which one may be lured. As the whole subject is of such importance, I propose to outline the procedure which it would normally be reasonably safe to follow.

When you are asked to give an open reference, that is, one which the person takes for future use, it is wiser to offer to supply one against an enquiry from an employer. There are, of course, instances where some form of recommendation is required for the purpose of showing to potential employers, and if the man or woman has been known to you over a number of years it would probably be safe to agree. You can do this without committing yourself to any statement which may have serious repercussions later.

Many references begin by stating the employee's length of service, the different kinds of work carried out, and so forth, but they are often too protracted and thereby lose much of their effect. The old custom of heading the statement: "To Whom It May Concern" need not be followed. All that is called for is a signed statement underneath a printed letter heading, somewhat as follows:

THE EUREKA TANDEM COMPANY LIMITED
Hanworth Works, Station Road
Coventry
West Midlands, CV7 8QQ

3 June 19XX

Mr Frank Wells has been employed by us as a Sales Manager for five years and we have found him to be honest. He is a man of great energy and considerable initiative. We believe that anything he undertakes will be carried out to the best of his ability.

(Signed)

TOMKINSON, DANIEL & TOMKINSON
3 Queen Square
Aberdeen, AB5 9XL

3 June 19XX

Miss Patricia Burke has been employed by us for the past two years as a shorthand-typist and we have found her to be entirely trustworthy. Her work has always been satisfactory.

(Signed)

In the event of an employer being asked for a testimonial by an untrustworthy or unsatisfactory employee, the safest reply is to explain that you have a general rule never to supply open references but will be pleased to answer any questions from future employers. On the other hand, it is always possible to give an innocuous letter on the following lines:

TOMKINSON, DANIEL & TOMKINSON
3 Queen Square
Aberdeen, AB5 9XL

3 June 19XX

Mr Thomas Blagdon has been with this firm as clerk for eighteen months and is leaving because he wishes to go abroad.

If an employee has been untrustworthy, it would be dangerous to give as brief a reference as the above, as it implies some degree of confidence where none, in fact, existed. When in doubt, it is generally wise to refuse to give your employee any sort of reference; there is no legal obligation to do so.

When handing an employee a satisfactory reference you are on reasonably safe ground, but if you make a statement somewhat on the following lines – "Miss A B Smith has been with us for five years and, *apart from her poor health*, has been quite satisfactory." – you might be courting serious trouble. Your statement might be held in law to be malicious libel. On the other hand, if you are answering an enquiry about it from a potential employer you are privileged and allowed comparatively wide scope, provided your reply *and the envelope* are marked "Private and Confidential". However, "the law is an ass", so you will be wise to give any adverse comments over the telephone or, more safely, by a personal discussion. Even telephone calls can be "tapped", and if you suspect that there are other listeners, be on your guard. Always remember that your comments, whether verbal or written, must be made in good faith. For example:

TOMKINSON, DANIEL & TOMKINSON
3 Queen Square
Aberdeen, AB5 9XL

28 July 19XX

PRIVATE AND CONFIDENTIAL
Mr Alfred J Shannon
Personnel Director
Shannon & Brewster Limited
Change Court
River Street
Aberdeen
AB9 5RT

Dear Mr Shannon

In reply to your enquiry of 26 July 19XX, concerning Miss May Hanworth, who has been employed by us for three months, we released her because we found her work to be generally unsatisfactory. She was inclined to be late for work on a number of occasions and caused a certain amount of trouble among the rest of our staff.

Yours sincerely

Andrew Smith

Admittedly, such a reference is extremely damning and would almost certainly jeopardise the girl's chances of obtaining a good post elsewhere, but your remarks - being, from your point of view, a true statement - could safely be committed to paper so long as they are marked "Private and Confidential" and are addressed to a senior official of the firm. Human nature being what it is, however, you would be wise to tone down your remarks as follows:

TOMKINSON, DANIEL & TOMKINSON
3 Queen Square
Aberdeen, AB5 9XL

28 July 19XX

PRIVATE AND CONFIDENTIAL
Mr Alfred J Shannon
Personnel Director
Shannon & Brewster Limited
Change Court
River Street
Aberdeen
AB9 5RT

Dear Mr Shannon

In reply to your enquiry of 26 July 19XX, concerning Miss May Hanworth, who has been employed by us for three months as a shorthand-typist, we are sorry to have to say that we did not find her suitable. Quite possibly she will do better with another employer.

Yours sincerely

Andrew Smith

Fortunately, most people know why they have been given notice, and they will probably try to avoid giving their last employers as a reference.

The Value of References

The only occasion where a reference is really of value is when the writer is known personally to the person for whom it is produced. An open reference under an unknown letter heading and over an equally unknown signature cannot be expected to carry much weight. Most people quite naturally like to give a good reference whenever they can, so that such open testimonials have of necessity lost much value.

It is never wise to send an *original* testimonial with an application; it might become lost or for some other reason you might never get it back. Always send a copy, marked accordingly. The original can be produced at a subsequent interview, but do not let it leave your possession.

Appointments

As a rule, these are simple and straightforward letters confirming verbal arrangements made at an interview.

In a book such as this I cannot deal fully with contracts of employment; sufficient to remark that such contracts are tricky for both sides. I remember a friend, and a solicitor at that, making a partnership contract with a sick old man of 80. My 47-year-old friend joined the old boy on a contract to work for nothing during the aged one's business life, thereafter he was to get the entire business for nothing. Result? My friend died at 60 while the old rascal was still in business at 93 and did not give my friend's widow a penny for 13 years of hard work!

The Contracts of Employment Acts

In July 1964 the original Act relating to Contracts of

Employment came into effect. Since that time it has been amended several times and new legislation introduced.

The aims of these Acts are to protect employees from unscrupulous practices and to make sure that all employers give employees full details, in writing, of their terms and conditions of employment. Written advice of pay increases/decreases must also be given to the employees as the changes occur.

Amongst the items that must be included in a Contract of Employment are: the minimum periods of notice to be given by both parties, as laid down by Parliament; the rate and frequency of pay, job title; hours of work; lunch break and other allowable breaks during the day; holiday entitlement and restrictions, if any; pension scheme provisions, sickness pay; disciplinary procedures and rules.

The Act covers part-time staff provided that they are working more than sixteen hours each week. However, part-time staff who have been continuously employed for more than five years are covered even if they work less than eight hours.

Official notes are available from the Department of Employment for the guidance of employers.

I now give an example of a letter offering employment.

SMITH & WILSON LIMITED
Hurstmoncieux Buildings, Vale Avenue
Blackpool, FY1 1DL

21 May 19XX

Mr D R J Black
13 Bedford Avenue
Blackpool
FY1 7DG

Dear Mr Black

We are writing to confirm our verbal arrangement that you should start work with us on 1 June 19XX, at 9 a.m., at a commencing salary of £xxx per week, subject to the standard conditions of employment laid down by Acts of Parliament, brief details of which you will find in the enclosed copy.

Please be kind enough to confirm this appointment.

Yours sincerely

J R Smith

The above example is a simple confirmation of appointment; but a special contract must be drawn up, embodying specific terms of service – this is dealt with on page 177, under 'Contracts'.

Resignations

As a rule, the acceptance of a resignation, on an official basis, is a simple matter and merely states the facts. I give first a specimen letter tendering a resignation and follow it with the official acceptance.

17 Daniel's Den
Hendon
London N7 9OL

28 June 19XX

Mr A Jones
Personnel Officer
The Britannia Engine Company Limited
Cheapside
London
EC8 6YY

Dear Mr Jones

On the recommendation of my medical adviser, I am regretfully obliged to tender my resignation from the staff of the Britannia Engine Company with effect from 31 July 19XX, and hereby give one month's notice in accordance with the terms of my contract.

Yours sincerely

John R Smith

THE BRITANNIA ENGINE COMPANY LIMITED
Cheapside, London, EC8 6YY

30 June 19XX

Mr John R Smith
17 Daniel's Den
Hendon
London
N7 90L

Dear Mr Smith

It is with regret that we accept your resignation from our staff, to take effect from 31 July 19XX. We are very sorry it has been necessary to take this step and hope that your health may soon improve.

Yours sincerely
THE BRITANNIA ENGINE COMPANY LIMITED

A Jones
Personnel Officer

Letters on similar lines may involve directors' or partners' resignations, or resignations from committees, clubs, societies and so forth.

Never write a letter of resignation (or indeed for any other purpose) *in the heat of the moment* and live to regret it. Make a draft, by all means, then leave it for a day or so. You may later change your mind, or circumstances may change it for you.

Letters on Retirement

When a director of a company, or a representative perhaps, retires it is often difficult to think of something nice to say which is just a little bit out of the ordinary, but which will be cherished by the recipient. What can be said of course depends very much on the circumstances, but a little bit of flattery goes down well and flattery can be true as well as false. Here is a sample:

JONES & SMITH LIMITED
48 Routlen Road
London, NW45 7JJ

23 September 19XX

Mr John Black
666 North Road
Wimbledon
SW19 7UU

Dear John

I find it very hard to believe you are retiring and I am sure you will have many interests which will fully occupy the leisure which you so much deserve.

Your company is losing a great asset. I remember the day when you arrived at our office to find us struggling with a burst pipe and how you helped us to bail out the water. Then there was the day when I took ill and at inconvenience to yourself you so kindly drove me 15 miles home.

But I will most remember you for all the useful and free advice you have offered us; it is not too much to say that we would not be where we are today if we hadn't accepted it.

Once again, wishing you every possible happiness in your retirement and hoping that if you ever pass our road you will come in for a chat.

Yours very sincerely
JONES & SMITH LIMITED

Richard Jones
Director

Letters of Congratulation

Such letters are often more difficult than they appear. You may have a *flair* for this type of letter and will in that case probably be in demand! Most business people will find a simple straightforward letter the easiest way of coping with the situation.

The custom of sending congratulatory letters has diminished in the last few years, although when someone wins public acclamation in a particular field, obtains academic distinction, becomes engaged or gets married, a message of goodwill and congratulation may be called for.

Engagements, marriages, births and business promotions generally present an occasion for a short letter, which may be on the following lines:

SIMPKIN & JONES LIMITED
Brush House, High Street
Bradford-on-Avon, Wiltshire, BA5 8UP

3 August 19XX

Mr J M Jackson
14 Roack Road
London
SW7 8UP

Dear Mr Jackson

I am delighted to hear of your new appointment to the Board. The many years you have worked with the Company have been rewarded, and my partner and I send you our very best wishes for the future.

Yours sincerely

J G Simpkin
Director

Keystone Hill
Kingston-upon-Thames, Surrey, KT1 6HA

29 September 19XX

Dear Mr Blagdon

I saw the announcement of the birth of your daughter in 'The Daily Telegraph' this morning, and I am writing to send my congratulations and best wishes to you and your wife.

I do hope your wife is progressing favourably and will soon be at home again.

Yours sincerely

Stephen Case

15–21 Tanner's Road
Blackheath
London, SW5 7YY

14 June 19XX

Sir Robert Keithley
Tower Chambers
West Street
London
WC1 7QQ

Dear Sir Robert

We were so pleased to see from the Honours List that your outstanding work as a Civil Engineer has been suitably rewarded, and send you our congratulations.

Yours sincerely

Geoffrey and Anne Masters

Letters of Sympathy

To convey sympathy sincerely but without falling into sentimentality needs thought.

Whilst it is admitted that sentimentality for its own sake must be avoided, some reference to the past is often called for and your aim must be to convey a genuine message of sympathy. It is not easy.

Chagford
Hill Top
Gloucester
GL16 0KK

22 April 19XX

Dear Mr Robinson

I have just heard with profound regret of your wife's death after a long illness. As you know, my wife and I enjoyed her friendship and hospitality on so many occasions that we feel her passing in a very personal sense and well understand how greatly you will miss her. You have our deepest sympathy.

Yours very sincerely

James Fitzgerald

KERR, BROWN & SONS LIMITED
Grand Arcade,
Felix Buildings, High Street
Greenford, Middlesex, UB6 9IP

24 October 19XX

Mr T R Black
Bloomfield & Pollard Limited
Porthouse
Queens Street
Manchester
M7 9OP

Dear Mr Black

We were distressed to read the announcement of Mr Pollard's death in this morning's 'Times', and write immediately to express our deep regret. By his untimely passing the computer industry has lost one of its pioneers. We recall his many kindnesses to our firm in the past, and we appreciate how much he will be missed by all who knew him and particularly by your numerous employees. He was a great man.

Yours very sincerely
KERR, BROWN & SONS LIMITED

Jonathan Jones
Director

Tor Hill
Sefton Road
Liverpool, L56 7UO

15 November 19XX

Mr W R Fulmer
Market Hospital
Little Gidding
Northampton
NN1 7UY

Dear Mr Fulmer

I was very sorry to hear, when I called at your office today, that you had been in the Rugby to London train accident, but equally relieved to learn that you are now making satisfactory progress and will be about again in a month's time.

In a long talk with your Manager I was told business is good and your firm has received a large number of orders for your new project. I shall be seeing him again next week and hope to hear that you are much better.

I expect to be in Northampton in a fortnight's time and hope to come and see you.

With kindest regards.

Yours sincerely

John Thompson

In many such instances, of course, one would use the Christian name. It is a custom I prefer, provided people know and like each other well.

10

LETTERS TO OFFICIALS

A letter to a Ministry or public servant should, of course, be quite a straightforward matter. Once it is despatched, you must be prepared to possess your soul in patience, for replies are often slow in coming.

Such letters may concern taxation, permits, licences, permissions and so forth. Some people seem to be much more successful in their dealings with authorities than others. Why is that? I think the answer is that the successful ones know more about how to approach the official mind. They marshall their facts in a way that appeals to bureaucratic instinct and tend to express their views in a factual and non-emotive way.

They display patience, persistence, courtesy, firmness and diplomacy, also sometimes flattery.

In this chapter, I give three examples of the sort of letter that you may sometimes have to write to officials. The first one concerns a planning application to build an office-block right outside my office window. The neighbour has applied for planning permission, and I am exercising my right to object to the application by writing to the Chief Planning Officer.

Planning Application No: 89/P0550
Re: Application by Messrs Jones, Jones & Smith to build a 3 storey office at 47 London Road, Lower Kingswood, Surrey. Objection from Elliot Right Way Books.

Dear Sir

1. Location

The premises of Elliot Right Way Books are shown on the site plan edged green, with the buildings edged blue. The applicant's site is edged yellow, with the proposed new office-block shown coloured pink.

2. Use of Buildings by Elliot Right Way Books

The existing buildings have windows on the south side at ground floor level only. These windows are of the offices used both for general office work and for proof-reading which is work requiring particularly good lighting. Two photographs are attached. The photograph marked (a) on the back shows exactly where the wall of the office-block would be in relation to our office window. This photograph is taken from point (a) on the plan. As will be seen, the office-block will take a large percentage of the light from the particular windows.

The photograph marked (b) is taken from point (b) on the plan, and shows the position of our windows in relation to the boundary line. In the event of planning permission being granted, we would have no alternative but to bring court proceedings for an injunction to restrain the erection of such a building by reason of its effect on our established rights of light. The legal advice we have received is that such an injunction would be granted.

3. Our Submission

Although we have our private legal remedies in respect of loss of light to our buildings, the consideration set out above is a material consideration for planning purposes, as confirmed by several recent court decisions. We therefore ask that full weight be given to this point in the determination of the application.

We urge that your authority should refuse permission for the development which has been proposed, and we look forward to receiving from you, in due course, notification of the Council's decision.

Yours faithfully

Planning departments generally treat reasonable local objections very sympathetically and such a letter would have a good chance of preventing a development which might otherwise easily be allowed.

The second example is a letter to the tax authorities in respect of someone whose tax code is wrong, and who is therefore suffering deduction of income tax when this should not be happening.

THE KING'S HEAD
North Road
Kingswood, Surrey
KT20 1AB

1 March 19XX

The Inspector of Taxes
Redhill 3 District
London Street North
Cardiff
CF2 8UP

Dear Sir

Re: Miss J Mitchell, Her National Insurance No. is WM 34 97 30A

Miss Mitchell works for us as a part-time barmaid on Friday nights and Saturday and Sunday lunchtimes only, and earns less than £xxx per week. She is in fact still a university student; she does not do any other work, and she has signed a statement to that effect on form P46 which we sent to you when she commenced employment two months ago.

Despite this, you have coded her on code 0, week one basis, and this means that we have to deduct income tax from her pay with no allowances at all.

Miss Mitchell informs us that she has complained to you on three separate occasions about this mis-coding, but she has never even received the courtesy of a reply. We are in the difficult position of being required by law to deduct tax on the basis of the code number which you have supplied for her, although we are well aware that she should not be suffering this tax deduction; in fact she is entitled now to a considerable refund.

Please will you therefore, as a matter of urgency, provide us with the correct code for Miss Mitchell, as a school-leaver in a first job with no other income. If your reply with the correct code is not received within the next seven days, we shall assist Miss

Mitchell in taking the matter up with our local Member of Parliament.

Yours faithfully

In the case of public servants who are totally unreasonable or incompetent, it is often found that a threat to place the matter in the hands of the local Member of Parliament will bring about a swift resolution of the problem.

The next letter concerns a staff member of otherwise good conduct who has unfortunately become embroiled in a fight outside the local pub in which someone was quite seriously injured. The young lad has been found guilty of Assault and will be sentenced after reports from the Social Services, Probation Officer, etc., have been taken into consideration. Since this person is a good employee who has never caused any problem at work, you wish to try to help him and could write to the Court as follows:

Clerk to the Justices

Dear Sir

We have been asked to write to you concerning the character of Mr John Smith who, we understand, has been found guilty of Assault.

Mr Smith has worked for us for the last

three years, ever since leaving school, and his duties include photography, plate-making and colour-origination for the printing industry.

We have found him to be a valuable and conscientious worker, and he is paid at the top rates for an apprentice of his age.

Mr Smith has a good job here and is highly regarded by all his colleagues. If he were to be sent to prison, he would lose the opportunity of securing a really good qualification in the printing industry and the excellent career that could follow for a man of his ability. If he were sent to prison, he could in fact very well become embarked upon a lifetime of crime, to the detriment both of himself and of society at large.

The circumstances of his conviction have been explained to us, and I must say that we find the story to be totally out of character with the John Smith that we know here. We feel sure that this aberrant behaviour results only from some uncharacteristic over-indulgence following his sister's engagement party.

While we are not in any way seeking to condone the seriousness of the crime that has been committed, we would nevertheless urge that in these particular circumstances the matter would be best dealt with by non-custodial means.

Yours faithfully

11

IMPORTANT LETTERS

I must begin this chapter with a strong warning. When you have an important letter to deal with – particularly one that entails a serious decision or a question of policy – do not be in a hurry. Remember, too, that letters can have consequences which may not be foreseen or intended by the sender. Therefore make it a firm rule that you should endeavour to call on the person concerned, if this is at all possible, so that you can talk the matter over. You are then on safer ground. Unfortunately, it is only too easy to be swayed by emotion and prejudice; people do not always approach their problems and difficulties in a scientific and detached way.

Timing

The importance of timing should be mentioned. In writing a policy or sales letter, for example, the date on which it is sent is often an essential factor. Imagine that circumstances have arisen whereby you decide to terminate an exclusive agency. Provided there is no fixed date by which notice must be given, it is obviously wise to wait for the right moment. If the contract involved an exclusive selling arrangement, it would be foolish to send the letter immediately after some large orders had been obtained. Business, goodwill and personal friendship are intermingled in the commercial world to an extent altogether beyond the appreciation of those outside it. To send your letter at such a time would probably create bitterness and justifiable anger, and a great deal of harm might ensue. And, lost goodwill.

On the other hand, if the letter is sent either after a quiet season or following a period during which business has been bad, the blow will be softened. Do not worry – unless your letter is urgent, it will not suffer by being delayed days, weeks or even (in extreme cases) months. Time often helps to clarify a situation. Naturally, any important decisions will have to be discussed with other partners or directors, and in most trades there are people (perhaps suppliers) of sound judgment who are generally willing to give their advice. Be careful, however, to choose a person whose confidence can be trusted. The advantage of a talk with someone outside the organisation is obvious: he can see the whole matter dispassionately and can bring a completely fresh mind to the subject. Such outside advice may not prove to be correct, but the discussion you have had may enable you to judge the best course to adopt.

More thought should be devoted to the timing of letters than is commonly given.

Prompt answers normally denote efficiency but often an acknowledgement, followed by delay, may be wiser. For instance, in quoting for work, the correct amount of delay could make the difference between getting the order and losing it. A ten-day wait could mean that all your competitors had got their prices in, so that when your representative called with the estimate, he held the advantage that the customer was ready to fix his order. One need not be a genius to be able to judge if one's price is right or too high. At the interview you can often sense if your estimate is out and make a small reduction to secure the order. Sometimes a phone talk before your quotation is sent will gain you valuable knowledge. Nine times in ten the last person to quote, if he is skilful, can get the job or at least the chance of it.

All successful companies pay attention to the timing of sales letters and publicity efforts, often striving to obtain nationwide or worldwide impact by co-ordinating several efforts at once.

It is always wise for the inexperienced to make a rough draft of their letter first; any omissions or alterations can be made before the final copy is drawn up.

You must try to get the right perspective by putting yourself in the place of the recipient. If you do not want to give him an opportunity to retaliate, be sure to word your letter in such a way that he cannot offer any reasonable argument. Diplomacy is nearly always necessary – for alternatives may exist which will not be altogether pleasant. But what is the secret of this diplomacy? Surely it is the ability to keep something up your sleeve so that you are not obliged to play your last card too early in your negotiations. Remember to avoid any tendency towards discourtesy, and appreciate the tremendous power of a polite answer to a discourteous letter.

I give below a few suggestions – with the qualification that they are only suggestions and there will be times when they must be ignored. In exceptional circumstances, drastic action may have to be taken.

1. Never post today what can be posted tomorrow.
2. There is a finality about the written word; respect it. Much can be said over a meal or even at an office meeting which would be unacceptable in a letter.
3. Try to judge the *effect* of your letter upon the recipient.
4. Listen to, but do not necessarily accept, the advice of people of ability and integrity.
5. Worry *before* you post your letter; once you have reached your decision, think no more about it. Remember, however, that having made your decision, you must abide by it and

take the consequences.

6. Make your letter absolutely clear. You may have to suffer for it, but there is no point in having to suffer because of a misunderstanding.
7. Avoid words like "ultimatum", "final decision" and so forth; you may have to eat them! If humanly possible, avoid promises at all times, and certainly all forms of threat, some of which may prove to be libellous.
8. There are occasions when letters are a better means of communication than even meetings; for example, they give time for the recipient to consider important points.

It is impossible to enumerate all the important matters which may require correspondence, but a few general examples are given below:

Questions of policy frequently cause difficulties. It may be decided, for instance, that the price of a certain model of bicycle will have to be raised substantially. A letter or circular to the trade, informing them bluntly of this advance in price might have a ruinous effect on business. Wherever it is possible to coat the pill with something palatable, do so. Some information might be included on a new advertising policy, the addition of new tools with the machine, or whatever it may be. These extra items may only account for £2 or so per bicycle, but the effect of giving the information with the price increase may well reduce the danger of competitors making too much capital out of your altered price.

A seller is sometimes unable to obtain orders from a certain buyer. His firm may feel that the latter is making a mistake in not purchasing his goods and may be tempted to write to the buyer's immediate superior or perhaps to the Managing Director, expressing uncomplimentary views on the buyer's judgment. The latter may be suspected of accepting bribes or of sheer incompetence; but a letter conveying this will not be easy to write, and could be extremely dangerous.

The first point to remember is that most employers have confidence in their staff, otherwise they would probably not retain them. Secondly, your accusations or suspicions may be impossible to prove. On the other hand, you may believe that, although little may be gained, nothing can be lost. An accusation of bribery constitutes a libellous statement and is dealt with in Chapter 5, but a letter informing the buyer's superior that you have found it impossible to sell to his firm's representative is in a different category.

Serious problems can often be overcome in quite a simple way. The difficulty might be solved by saying to the buyer: "Do you mind if I send a sample to your Managing Director? I have a feeling he might disagree with you about the value of our goods." By watching his reaction, you will be able to judge whether or not he is sure of his ground. If all else fails and it is decided to go over his head, try to do so in the least obvious way. The following letter will give some indication of a line which might be adopted:

SMITH & JONES LIMITED
Territorial Buildings
Bath Street
Chatham, Kent, ME6 7UY

5 August 19XX

PRIVATE AND CONFIDENTIAL
The Managing Director
Excelsior Goods Limited
45 Henchurch Street
Ilford
Essex
IG7 6QQ

Dear Sir

Our representative has been calling regularly in an endeavour to introduce our new "Cut-Clean" Lawn Mower to your company, but we have not so far been able to interest your buyer in the proposition. We have already pointed out that we feel he is making a mistake in not giving this machine a trial, and have also mentioned to him that we would be writing to you as we are sure our machines merit full consideration by you.

The "Cut-Clean" Lawn Mower costs £xxx, which includes delivery to any of your branches, and confidentially, on an initial order we are prepared to allow you an extra ten per cent discount. Our reason for writing to you is that we did not wish to mention the granting of this discount to your buyer as we are anxious that it should be treated in the strictest confidence.

We hope to hear that we may send you a machine for trial purposes.

Yours faithfully
SMITH & JONES LIMITED

K Smith

Let us take another fairly straightforward example. A U.K. agent representing an American timber shipper offers you a carload of extra wide Prime Quality Cottonwood. He makes this offer verbally and says he is willing to leave it with you for forty-eight hours. On the second day you telephone to accept the material at that price but the agent informs you he has sold the consignment twenty-four hours previously and has received five dollars more than he quoted you. This is obviously sharp practice, but the agent (presumably as there is nothing in writing) feels legally safe. In certain circumstances he may be, but in this particular case his position is by no means secure. Firstly, extra wide Cottonwood is a rarity; secondly, he had given away certain information – namely, that he had sold the wood for five dollars more than he originally quoted you. It is a custom of the timber trade that agents work for a commission, so that, in this instance, the price originally quoted must have been given to him by his principal in America. Your evidence might be based on an offer you had made, by letter, to a provincial buyer. In other words, if you could produce a copy of your offer and a letter from your customer confirming telephone acceptance within forty-eight hours, you would have an almost watertight case. Such a case, however, would be extremely difficult to fight in law and would, of course, require expert and expensive legal advice.

Probably a more effective way would be, firstly a direct approach to the agent in his office, with a statement that you intended to put the whole matter before his shipper unless he did something about it. As a result, he might give you a letter to the effect that you would receive the next offer of this specification available, in which case you would have won a very good point. If, however, he proved unco-operative, this would afford an excellent opportunity to "go over his head" by writing to his principal, explaining the situation – which would probably get the agent into fairly serious trouble and might even jeopardise his agency. But mark your letters and envelopes "Private and Confidential".

Normally life is too short to go to such a lot of trouble, but circumstances occasionally arise where a stand has to be made – a stand, possibly, largely for the sake of the integrity of the business world – and I have accordingly outlined a suggested course.

Sample letter to American shipper, to fit the circumstances described above, might be as follows:

ELLIOT & ELLIOT
12–16 Mersham Street
Crewe, Cheshire, CW1 2XB

15 August 19XX

Private & Confidential

The President
J & A Winning Cartwright Inc.
1214 East Central Avenue
New York
NY 1000
USA

Dear Sir

Two days ago we received a firm offer from your agent for extra wide Prime Cottonwood at $700 per unit. Your agent made this offer firm for forty-eight hours, and we enclose a copy of our letter to our own customer, Messrs Benjamin Powell & Rankin Ltd, Tenby Road, Liverpool. You are, of course, at liberty to refer to them for confirmation should you so desire. We hold their Order Number 3501 for the goods in question confirming their telephone order.

When we approached your agent well within the forty-eight hours, however, we were informed that the Cottonwood had been sold to a third party at five dollars more than was quoted to us. We regard this as a serious breach of faith on the part of your agent, and as you will appreciate, it has put us in an extremely awkward position with our customer.

We would ask whether you can supply us with another carload of the same specification at as early a date as possible? We much regret having had to write to you direct, but you will understand there was no other course open to us.

Yours faithfully

A letter couched in these terms is, of course, a very serious matter as the evidence it contains might jeopardise the agent's position. It also contains information which, if it reached the agent's hands, might result in his taking action against you. Such an action would probably be based on a charge of defamation of character on the grounds that the agent had not in fact made you any firm offer. Your customer's confirmatory order, however, would provide circumstantial evidence, and the fact that your letter to the shipper was headed "Private and Confidential" should enable you to enjoy reasonable safety. Before such a letter is posted – and this applies to all similar cases – it is safer to obtain legal advice. But always remember that legal advice *can* be wrong. Personally, I should risk such a letter without fear, if the need arose.

Registration

All vitally important letters should be sent by Registered or Recorded Delivery post, to provide evidence that the letter has been delivered and signed for on receipt. If necessary – certain circumstances may demand this – a spare copy of the registered letter can be dispatched by ordinary post the following day for double safety.

A confirmation of receipt should be watched for by return or within a few posts. Bear in mind registered letters normally take longer in the post.

Do not register letters that are not of sufficient importance to merit this precaution. In my experience, there are few things so irritating as to open a registered letter only to find it contains information of no consequence.

12

ORDERS AND CONFIRMATORY LETTERS

Declining Orders

In commerce there are times when, owing to circumstances – weather, perhaps, or sudden runs on stock – orders must be declined because the demand for certain goods exceeds the supply. This situation needs careful handling because buyers are easily offended and many of them seem to think they have only to demand something to get it.

A polite acknowledgement of the request should be sent of which the following is an example:

GREENWOOD & SONS LIMITED
Unit 5
Singer Street Industrial Estate
Warrington, Cheshire, WA5 6UU

9 April 19XX

For the attention of Mr J G Brown
J G & D Brunton Limited
Cornhill Chambers
South Street
Preston
Lancashire
PR4 8UY

Dear Sir

Thank you very much for the order received this morning for 30 pairs of suede gloves. We much regret, however, that our stock of these particular gloves is now exhausted and it is not expected that further supplies will be available for some weeks. The moment we can let you have a definite order, we will contact you.

Yours faithfully
GREENWOOD & SONS LIMITED

H A Stephenson

If, however, you happen to know of anyone who holds a stock of the goods in question, it is always helpful to give their name and address – a small service which may later be remembered.

A letter declining to fulfil an order because the enquirer's account has not been paid is more difficult. An "Either/Or" ultimatum is almost certain to result in giving offence; something rather more diplomatic is called for. For example:

GREENWOOD & SONS LIMITED
Unit 5
Singer Street Industrial Estate
Warrington Cheshire, WA5 6UU

2 January 19XX

Strictly Private and Confidential

The Manager
Webber & John Limited
71 Cheapside
London
EC3G 4FX

Dear Sir

Many thanks for sending us your order number 123, but as your account is somewhat overdue and now exceeds £5000, we would appreciate a cheque from you before we can enter into further transactions.

We know how difficult conditions are just now, but we have many commitments of our own to meet. If, therefore, you are able to send us a cheque for £2500 in part payment of your account, we shall be most grateful. It will then be possible to supply you with a further quantity of goods.

Yours faithfully
GREENWOOD & SONS LIMITED

H A Stephenson

The wording of this letter will depend upon the decision reached as to how much the customer is to be asked to pay.

In any refusal to quote, similar courtesy should be shown as it is this sort of thing which builds up the goodwill of a business. It is perhaps hardly necessary to mention that a firm should always quote, if humanly possible (provided there are no financial reasons against this policy), even if it means obtaining a product from a competitor. If such a reputation is once established, general enquiries are more likely to be received.

When quotations are made on behalf of competitors, the profit margin must obviously be small, and unless it is sufficient it will be unwise to incur the risks involved. As I have already stressed, however, it is a sound policy to quote whenever you can.

Judging Integrity by the Letter Heading

It is never safe to judge the standing of a correspondent from the appearance of his letter heading. A dishonest firm may take tremendous trouble with its notepaper; and equally, some perfectly trustworthy businessmen take no trouble whatever. Speaking generally, however, it is true that if a letter heading has been attractively laid out, giving the names of the partners or directors and all other essential information, it is often reasonably safe to assume that the firm is reliable. The information given can, of course, be checked if necessary to ensure that it is genuine.

Most firms possess trade directories and lists of customers going back some years. If, for example, the name of a firm appeared two or three years ago and is still on the current lists, that fact should stand in their favour. Sometimes, by judging the quantity of goods asked for in relation to the size of the town or village and *the way the letter is worded*, you can make a reasonably accurate guess as to the integrity of the enquirer. With experience, this becomes almost instinctive.

Dealing with Errors

When an error is detected, it is vital to deal with it immediately. Goods of the wrong size may be delivered, for example, or they may have been damaged in transit; an invoice may have been wrongly charged or calculated. The possibilities of error are unlimited and can only be reduced to the minimum by efficient organisation.

Certain firms have a strict rule that claims must be made within a limited period – seven days, fourteen days, or even by return of post; so act at once. You could telex or fax your claim to your supplier or use the telephone to let him know and then send a written confirmation as well (keeping a copy for your records). These initial letters are not usually difficult to write; it is simply a case of writing to explain the exact position, and the secret of success – if it is a secret – is courtesy and (if need be) firmness. A sample letter in illustration is given below:

W & T BROWN LIMITED
14 The Arcade
High Street, Manchester, M6 7KK

23 September 19XX

Harvey & Sankey Limited
Central Buildings
North Road
Liverpool
L5 7UP

Dear Sirs

We are returning your invoice for the twelve woollen cardigans charged at £xxx each, which we assume is an error. This sale was made to the undersigned by your representative and the price quoted was £xx each cardigan.

We shall be glad if you will confirm this and make the necessary alteration to the invoice. The goods are of no use to us at the higher price. An early satisfactory reply will enable us to start selling them.

Yours faithfully
W & T BROWN LIMITED

S T Jones
Manager

Do not in any circumstances write as follows:

W & T BROWN LIMITED
14 The Arcade
High Street, Manchester, M6 7KK

23 September 19XX

Harvey & Sankey Limited
Central Buildings
North Road
Liverpool
L5 7UP

Dear Sirs

We have your invoice and fail to understand why you have added £xx to the price quoted by your representative. We regard this as extremely sharp practice and shall be glad if you will correct the invoice immediately.

Yours faithfully
W & T BROWN LIMITED

S T Jones
Manager

Not only is this a most unlikely way of achieving anything but it is almost sure to result in an answering letter which might lead to trouble varying from insistence that you should keep the goods at the full £xxx to the possibility of legal action. There will in any case be much unpleasant argument.

A good deal of psychology must be used in letter writing. Avoid at all costs this type of letter which comes from a builder to his timber merchant:

JONES & SMITH LIMITED
5 Hele Road
Birmingham, B5 8QY

4 April 19XX

Forrest Turnbull & Company Limited
Farnham Street
Nuneaton
Warwickshire
CV7 9OP

Dear Sirs

Your lorry driver delivered 24 boards extra wide oak to our yards this morning. Three of these boards, however, contained large knots, although the wood was understood to be of prime quality when ordered.

We have sent the wood back to you, carriage forward, and return your invoice herewith.

Yours faithfully
JONES & SMITH LIMITED

J Jones

If you put yourself in the timber merchant's position, you will understand why he is likely to be annoyed. In all probability, the goods were shipped in good faith and the mistake was made quite unwittingly, and he will have paid carriage on the boards. Although it may be necessary to insist that he takes them back ultimately, there is always the possibility that the matter can be put right and some allowance made on the faulty material. If, however, such material is useless to you at any price, it is wiser to write a courteous letter first, explaining what has happened and asking what arrangements the merchant is prepared to make. This gives the latter the chance to save double carriage, as he may have another customer nearby who would be willing to co-operate by taking the first delivery from you.

Unnecessary Letters

I have already mentioned the importance of avoiding unnecessary correspondence. Few things are likely to irritate a businessman more than letters enclosing invoices, statements and receipts, and letters acknowledging small orders – particularly as the goods probably arrive by the same post.

Nevertheless, there are certain items which do require confirmation; for instance, important telephone calls. Important conversations or decisions should always be confirmed in writing and a copy retained. If this is not done, considerable confusion may later arise. Some business people do not confirm important decisions in this way and in dealing with men of integrity it may be, and usually is, perfectly all right, but the trouble is not only the danger of failing memories but the death of senior officials – and this may lead to serious complications later. In your endeavour to prove your point you may only arouse suspicion in others who do not understand the position if the matter has not been confirmed by letter.

13

PUBLICITY AND SALES LETTERS

Publicity Letters

As its name implies, the purpose of the publicity letter is to obtain publicity for a cause, for a campaign or for merchandise.

As publicity is often a substitute for advertising, and since the latter costs money, it can readily be understood why such publicity is difficult to obtain without involving a certain amount of expense. Editors of papers, magazines and other similar media are constantly on the watch to prevent free publicity being obtained, thereby saving the insertion of a *pro rata* advertisement.

Without going into the technicalities of research on the subject, the importance of publicity is (generally speaking) in direct relation to the reader potential of the medium selected. Thus, to give a simple example, a man selling a product suitable for agricultural use will benefit from publicity in a farming magazine rather than by a display advertisement in a political magazine.

The mention you read in the evening paper about the acreage of orchards owned by a certain cider manufacturer may have been inserted because the editor or journalist considered the information to be of general interest, but more probably it was inserted because the public relations department of the cider farm was able to convince the editor that the matter was of wide appeal.

Again, human nature being what it is, if the firm in question does a lot of advertising in that particular paper, it is possibly correct to suppose that the editor will imagine any information coming from them to be of more general interest than is in fact the case. Not every publication operates on 100% editorial integrity.

Your best chance of success lies in possessing something that is outstanding in itself and of genuine interest to the public. Remember that the greater the interest you can create, the greater the chance of your particular form of publicity being accepted. To cite an obvious example: a steel manufacturer wishes to increase the use to which his materials can be put and he accordingly initiates a correspondence in the press to the effect that steel should be used in the construction of houses as it is non-inflammable. There is a chance that a timber producer will reply by pointing out that timber can be proofed against fire and that it is much cheaper than steel – each side seeking opportunities for publicity.

You may read that X, the famous film star, has driven a golf ball 250 yards during an International Match at Beverly Hills, California. This statement is probably publicised to draw attention to the film star rather than to his prowess as a golfer, and it is more than likely that his agent has had a hand in it.

The following gives an example of some publicity issued on behalf of a world-famous jockey, who is on the eve of retirement and whose life story is to be published within a few days. A letter is sent to the editor of a sporting paper with a wide circulation, in the following terms:

Borrowness
Green Fields
Newmarket, CB1 8UP

4 October 19XX

Mr P I Lansell
The Editor
The Sporting Argus
1 Bishopsgate
London
EC4 7UY

Dear Mr Lansell

It occurs to me that you may care to make some reference to one of this country's leading jockeys, John Smith, who is retiring after over thirty years in the saddle.

It is probably not generally known that out of 3,000 races, he has ridden over 700 winning horses and has taken second place in nearly 1,000 races of first-class importance. John will surely be chiefly remembered, however, for his kindness to less fortunate riders and for the unceasing help he has given to the Jockeys' Benevolent Society.

Many of John's admirers will look forward to reading his new book "Keep Your Tail Up", which is to be published on 10 October by Webb & Lockey. In it, much autobiographic information has been included which will appeal not only to turf lovers but also to readers interested in the outstanding figures of the racing world.

Yours sincerely

A press release, giving more detailed information about the book, would also be sent with this letter.

Publicity letters call for endless thought and care if they are to succeed, but it is also easy to over-rate the importance of publicity, for if too much money or time is spent on it, there is less to devote to other and equally important matters.

The Sales Letter

All business executives connected with marketing should be able to write effective sales letters. For some products it will only be necessary to write: "We have pleasure in offering the following:", thereafter listing the individual items, but for others something more will be required. Many letters are damned from the outset by being too long, and the reader becomes bored; alternatively, they are ruined by not being sufficiently explicit. Put yourself in the buyer's place and assess the advantage he would derive from your goods or services, and in your letter come straight to the point and try to show him scientifically and logically why he should have them. Other factors – friendship, sympathy and so on – can play their part, particularly between people who have known one another for a considerable time.

Two examples of sales letters are given overleaf: first a "negative" letter and second a "positive" one which is much better:

WOOD & KING LIMITED
Unit 15
Tallent Road
Harborne
Birmingham, B65 7KL

25 January 19XX

The Manager
W S Palmer Limited
18 West Street
Horley
Surrey
RH5 8QP

Dear Sir

I am writing to make you an offer of our new electronic cash register at £xxx each. Many of our customers have told us how much they like these machines, which are well built and carry with them our One Year Guarantee.

We shall be pleased to arrange for our local representative to call upon you with a machine for trial purposes at any time convenient to you.

Yours faithfully
WOOD & KING LIMITED

A C Wood

WOOD & KING LIMITED
Unit 15
Tallent Road
Harborne
Birmingham, B65 7KL

25 January 19XX

Mr J K Mitchell
The Manager
W S Palmer Limited
18 West Street
Horley
Surrey
RH5 8QP

Dear Mr Mitchell

Our representative was passing your shop last Monday when you were out, and noticed that your assistant was ringing up the goods on an old-fashioned manual cash register. We appreciate that this is fairly general practice in small shops, but wondered if you knew how much time could be saved by using the more modern electronic cash registers?

We have spent many years of research in perfecting the latest type of electronic cash register and we now feel that we have found the answer. Our machines may appear more expensive at the outset, but the extra cost will be more than saved in time and wages. Thanks to the advance of technology in this field in recent years, the cost of these machines has greatly decreased.

Some machines are now so sophisticated that they can keep stock control records, while others use a credit card payment system. Three of our machines are at present in use in a local chemist's shop, and the manager would be happy to answer any questions you might wish to put to him. Our machines are guaranteed for one year but they are likely to give at least ten years' excellent service.

A trial order will be most gratefully received, or our local representative will gladly call and give a demonstration without obligation.

Yours sincerely
WOOD & KING LIMITED

A C Wood

Circulars, Press Releases and Direct Mail Letters

A circular or press release can be sent to announce a social event, can contain up-to-the-minute market reports and information to shareholders, or, of course, can announce a company's new product.

Today, with the advance of computers and word processors, businesses can also send out more "personalised" advertising material. Letters can be written and addressed to individual customers, thereby giving a better impression. However, so many of these direct mail letters are sent out nowadays that many customers barely glance at them before filing them in the waste paper bin!

Firms with a large mail often find it economical to frank their own envelopes; this provides an opportunity to advertise, perhaps, your own trademark or brand.

14

FOREIGN MAIL

Business letters to overseas correspondents must possess the same qualities as those intended for home "consumption", though they may require greater *expertise*. There are several points to remember.

First, the recipient is several hundred miles away, and if your letter is not clearly expressed he will be faced with difficulties which he cannot immediately clear up. He may have to telephone you to clarify the matter.

Secondly, there is the difficulty of language. Even though your correspondent may be in an English-speaking country, always use *plain* English and avoid slang terms or any words which are not in common use. The chances of being misunderstood are otherwise intensified. In England, for example, we call an "apartment" a "flat", and "pants" are described as "trousers". Unfortunately, both these words mean entirely different things in America! In that country, for instance, sweets are called "candy", and biscuits "crackers".

Ideally, of course, men and women handling foreign mail should have lived for some time in the country concerned, or at least have visited it, so that they can appreciate the finer points of custom and usage, but a possible substitute is to read books and magazines published in that country so that your own approach becomes less insular and acquires the right "slant".

Fundamentally, foreign mail is dealt with in much the same way as home correspondence, but letters which may take weeks to reach their destination must be written with that fact in mind. Letters which are to be sent by air mail can be written on very thin paper, or, of course, the air mail letter form, so that the weight is reduced to a minimum.

Letters going to countries with unfamiliar alphabets (e.g. China, Japan, Greece, Soviet Union, and Arab countries) should have the envelopes typed in CAPITALS, or written in block capitals.

15

BUSINESS TERMS, PHRASES AND ABBREVIATIONS

The use of many expressions and terms current in business is, outside certain well-defined limits, to be deprecated. It becomes, in fact, one of those forms of laziness of which we are all guilty.

One of the problems is that different terms apply in different parts of the country or world, even in the same trade, and confusion is likely to arise if some abbreviations are used. This underlines a very important rule: make sure that everything you write is clear.

The letters *E & OE* are seen on quotations, invoices, etc., and stand for an important safeguard: *Errors and Omissions Excepted.* Curiously enough, it is not so often seen today, and I personally deplore its absence as it provides an honourable retreat in the event of a blunder.

Cif stands for *cost, insurance and freight.* If I ask a firm in America to quote me for one ton of cotton, cif Tilbury, his price to me includes the cost of the cargo, the insurance and the freight – the last two of which he pre-pays. Delivery would be alongside the dock at Tilbury. Unloading charges would be my concern or – to use another business phrase – "for my account".

for means *free on rail*, that is, free delivery as far as the *consignor's* railway station or depot.

fob: *free on board*, that is, delivered to the ship.

b/l: *bill of lading*, that is, a bill of authority for shipping merchandise by sea.

Dy and d/d: *delivery* and *delivered*, but these words should be written out in full.

Bulk delivery: delivery only in large quantities.

Each trade has, of course, a host of expressions applicable to its own business, and whilst I do not intend to deal with the hundreds of specialised terms in this book, here is a list of a few of them, together with foreign phrases which may be met:

List of Some Terms Used in Business

a/c	account
ack.	acknowledge
ad fin.	near or towards the end
ad hoc	for this purpose
ad infinitum	to infinity
ad lib. (ad libitum)	as much as you like; without control
ad referendum	for further consideration
ad valorem (A/V)	based on value – sometimes a Customs & Excise term (or an import duty)
addendum	an additional remark to be added
antedate	dated earlier than arranged
AOB	any other business
a/r	all risks
b/e	bill of exchange; also bill of entry (for Customs)
b/f	brought forward (accounts)
bhp	brake horse power (engineering)
b/l	bill of lading
bleed	the part of an illustration which runs off the page (printing)
Btu	British thermal unit
c/a	current account
CA	Chartered Accountant (Scotland)
c & f	cost and freight
carr. pd.	carriage paid
caveat emptor	let the buyer beware
c/c	centre to centre (measurement)

c.d. (cum dividend)	with the dividend to come
c/f	carried forward (accounts)
cif	cost, insurance and freight
c/o	care of
c.o.d.	cash on delivery
contra	against; opposite (as "contra a/c")
corrigendum	item, word or line to be corrected
cr.	credit or creditor
cu.	cubic
cv	curriculum vitae (life/career history)
cwo	cash with order
D/d	delivered
de facto	in fact
de jure	by right
del credere	risk of a bad debt
dr.	debit or debtor
D.V. (Deo volente)	God willing
D.V. & W.P.	God willing and weather permitting
Dy	Delivery
E & OE	Errors and Omissions excepted
e.g. (exempli gratia)	for example
et al.	and elsewhere
et seq.	and following
etc. (etcetera)	and others
ex	from (as "ex stock")
ex. div.	exclusive of dividend
ex officio	by virtue of office
excl.	exclusive or excluding
fait accompli	an accomplished fact
FAO	for the attention of
fas	free alongside ship
FCA	Fellow of the Institute of Chartered Accountants (England and Wales)
fob	free on board } buyer pays freight after
for	free on rail } put on ship or rail
force majeure	over-riding circumstances, act of God, etc. (whereby a contract may be cancelled or varied)
ft	foot or feet
ft cu	cubic foot or feet
hors de saison	out of season
i.e. (id est)	that is
Inc.	Incorporated (USA equivalent of "limited")
in extenso	at full length
in extremis	at the extreme point
in situ	in position
in status quo	in the original state
in toto	in full
inst.	instant; the present (month)
inter alia	among other matters
inv.	invoice
I.O.U.	I owe you – a promise to repay money, the

	amount to be stated, signed but not dated
ipso facto	by that very fact
l/c	letter of credit
Ltd.	Limited
modus operandi	method of operation
MP	Member of Parliament
mpg	miles per gallon
mph	miles per hour
ms and mss	manuscript and manuscripts
mv	motor vessel
NB (nota bene)	note well
ne plus ultra	none better
nem. con. (nemine contradicente)	without opposition
non seq.	it does not follow
o/a	on account
o/c	overcharge
o/d	overdraft or overdrawn
OHMS	On His/Her Majesty's Service
OK	correct (slang, but now generally recognised)
onus	responsibility
%	per cent or per hundred
op	out of print
O/S	outstanding; also out-size
PA	per annum, yearly; also Personal Assistant
per	by
per diem	by the day
Plc	public limited company
pod	proof of delivery
post-date	to date in advance – a later date
pp	per pro (on behalf of); also pages
prima facie	as far as first appears – on the face of it
pro	for
pro forma	as a matter of form (pro forma invoice, one calling for cash in advance)
pro rata	proportionately
pro tem.	for the time being
prox. (proximo)	next (month)
PS	post scriptum – written afterwards; an afterthought
PSI	per square inch
qv (quod vide)	which see
R.D.	refer to drawer (e.g. a cheque which a bank will not meet)
rep.	representative
rpm	revolutions per minute
RSJ	rolled steel joist (constructional engineering)
RSVP	please reply
rwh	rainwater head (building)
rwp	rainwater pipe (building)
seriatim	serially, one after the other
sine die	indefinitely

sine qua non	a necessity
sq.	square
status quo	existing condition
std.	standard
stet	let it stand; leave as before
sub judice	under consideration, not yet settled in court
swg	standard wire gauge (engineering)
T & G	tongued and grooved (timber)
TG & V	tongued, grooved and V-jointed (timber)
tel quel	quality offered just as it is
trs.	transpose
ult. (ultimo)	last (month)
ultra vires	beyond one's powers
VAT	Value Added Tax
verb sap.	a word to the wise is sufficient
verbatim	word for word
via	by way of
vice versa	the other way round
vide	see
viz	namely
w/e	week ending
wef	with effect from
wfi	wait for it
wg	wire gauge
W.P.	word processing; weather permitting
wpb	waste paper basket
wt	weight
∴	therefore

Metric Measures

cc	cubic centimetre
cm	centimetre
g or gm	gram(me)
kg	kilogram(me)
l	litre
m	metre
ml	millilitre
mm	millimetre
tonne	metric ton

16

CONTRACTS AND EMPLOYMENT AGREEMENTS

General Remarks

Sufficient importance is rarely attached to contracts or agreements, and the first point I wish to emphasise is that no one should ever sign anything of this nature without reading and understanding it. This sounds childish advice, but I have known otherwise astute men and women who have signed a document unread and lived to regret it bitterly. Contracts or agreements may have long-term results, and, even if entered into through a misunderstanding, are usually irrevocable. The law is frequently an ass but it does have the power of the courts behind it, and indeed, life would not be possible without an undertaking being enforceable. Let rule one be, *read and understand before you sign*.

A contract usually affects two (or more) people or parties, and if all were honourable and reasonable a wrongly worded clause would doubtless matter little, as it could be rectified by a new agreement. Unfortunately, in business as elsewhere, there exist people who try to take advantage.

On several occasions I have known instances where contracts for merchandise or services were drawn up on the understanding that the wording was the same as in a previous similar contract. Now, it is time-consuming to read again every clause of a long contract which is supposed to be word for word as before, yet, through not having done so, I have known people to find themselves in the most difficult position. One of the parties had slipped in a word or a clause which was not identical with the previous contract and which altered its meaning. In other words, the contract was obtained by sharp practice. So, at the risk of repetition, do not forget rule one – read and understand before you sign.

Were such an unfortunate thing to happen to you, it is, of course, possible that by visiting the dishonest party and "having it out" a fresh contract could be obtained and the "incorrect" one destroyed. It is also possible that if the other party refused to put the matter right, a lawyer could advise you how to escape the dread consequences of your folly by taking advantage of some weak clause in the contract which would make the whole thing unworkable. Were this not possible, if by your carelessness you had signed something which was going to have a serious effect on your life, quite likely it would be worthwhile threatening, or even going so far as to take the matter to court. If the word or words which had been inserted without your knowledge were unreasonable and such as no reasonable person would sign, and if you could swear on oath that the other party had assured you the contract was identical with a previous one between you, my guess is that the Court would declare the second contract null and void. But my guess may be wrong, and in every court battle both sides think they will win, or they would pull out beforehand, and *one side always loses* – remember that before going to law.

I do not wish to leave this vital rule one, *Read and Understand*, until I have hammered it thoroughly, at the risk of your being annoyed with me, into your conscious and subconscious mind, because once you have really grasped it you are fairly safe.

Understanding is most important. A promise made verbally, or in an exchange of letters could easily be just as enforceable as a contract. True, in a verbal promise, if there is no witness, it might be difficult for the other party to enforce the terms, but often it is less difficult than one might think. Another equally vital rule, then, is to be very careful what you do promise. Indeed, one of my business mottoes is "promise as little as you can, but carry out all you do undertake". Remember, make as few definite promises as possible, for they all have to be fulfilled.

Understanding the terms of a contract is often difficult. To give a simple example which comes to mind: I remember a contract which was fixed in January with the shipment date July/August/September. A few days after the contract was made, the buyer asked to have it altered as he found he could not accommodate the earlier shipment dates and he inserted "Shipment: not before September". In his mind he wanted to make sure the goods did not leave in July or August but in September. The shipper, thousands of miles away, apparently read the contract otherwise – intentionally or unintentionally, I do not know – with the outcome that he did not ship until the following December. The buyer could do nothing and had to accept delivery although the material was too late for the job and he was forced to buy at a high price in the open market to fill his order from his own customer, and was subsequently landed with a shipment of specially-cut material which was useless to him. He lost thousands of pounds.

I remember another contract in which an author, in exchange for a considerable advance, was to deliver a manuscript "when complete", no date being mentioned for completion. Need I add it was never delivered and the publisher lost his advance money? The particular author was a crook, and this brings me to the subject of dealing with people lacking in integrity.

No one is clever enough to deal with dishonest people and get away with it for long; the man who is out to "do" you will almost certainly succeed in the end. He spends his time working out clauses which enable him to escape, but which are so worded that you are likely not to notice the weakness in the wording. Avoid, therefore, as far as possible, all contracts with those who are dishonest, however profitable a deal may appear on the face of it.

Many contracts can be "legally" broken and that is why, although every care should be exercised to make the wording clear and straightforward, it is far better to bank upon the integrity of the person with whom you deal, than on his actual contract. It is because of this that we have the saying: "You can drive a horse and cart through any contract", although it is only partly true.

Many people imagine that lawyers can draw up foolproof contracts, but a little thought will show that this is not so. A lawyer cannot possibly understand the intricacies of every trade and whilst he may be able to help the inexperienced in drafting clauses, he may omit or overlook some important point; so much is this so that I consider a solicitor, for this type of work, unless he has special experience in the particular field, to be almost useless. As an adviser he may be helpful, but probably less so that some experienced business colleague.

Owing to all the different terms and customs in each trade, I can do little more than give brief outlines here and sound warnings of a general nature.

In this question of understanding, we should be clear what the contract is. It is little more than the setting down, as a permanent record and reference, the terms or conditions which have been agreed between the parties, often after long negotiation and discussion in which give-and-take usually play an important part. The contract is necessary because it saves the memory, and should any of the contracting parties die or retire, acts as a guide to those who follow. If a business is sold, its existing contracts are extremely important and valuable.

The wording should be straightforward. It is not necessary, and indeed it is not "done" today to use big words and legal phrases if ordinary English can be employed. For the normal business contract, legal advice is usually not necessary, but I must say that although I have perused many contracts, I have hardly ever seen a properly worded one. This is, I think, due to the habit of not bringing the wording up-to-date to fit new conditions, many firms using the same old style which served their predecessors well. I will give an example of what I regard as poor wording which I have seen in the publishing trade. "The price of the book will be £20 net and the rate of royalty shall be £2 per copy." This is possibly perfect wording so far as the first edition of the book is concerned, but perceive what an awkward position the publisher has put himself into should the book become a best-seller and go into many editions year after year. Due to rising costs it might no longer be possible for the firm to sell the book at £20 and it might be necessary to raise the price to £30. If the author is fair, it should be easy enough to obtain his agreement, either by a new contract or by exchange of letters, which is as legal, that the price should be £30 and the royalty rate £3 (which is the same percentage), but what could happen is that the author disagrees, or perhaps he or she has died and the widow or widower is an unreasonable person, so that the publisher is faced with the probability of losing the rights of publishing the book to some competing firm who will enjoy all the spade work he has done in establishing it.

If he had worded the original clause as follows he would not be in this predicament:

"The Publisher expects the price of the book will be £20 for the first edition, but the question of price for the first or any subsequent editions (if any) shall be left entirely to the discretion of the publisher, and the royalty rate *shall be ten per cent* of the net published price."

Of course, there might have to be special clauses about a lower rate of royalty should a paperback book be published, or a cheap edition, or should the book be remaindered, and so on, but I am only using the one clause as illustration of the care which is essential.

I am anxious to stress that those who draw up contracts must think hard of all possibilities and difficulties which may arise, and protect themselves against being "caught out" by some change of circumstances. Clarity is not enough; foresight is also required.

British commerce has been built up on the saying that an "Englishman's word is his bond" and "The integrity of the City of London is second to none throughout the world". Let me then repeat, when you do make any promise, fulfil it, but do try and avoid making undertakings which it may be impossible to carry out. Politicians make vague promises for electioneering and other purposes, which they have no intention of implementing, but do not let the business world demean itself by following their example. Commerce depends upon integrity, and without it the wheels of industry could not function smoothly.

Each party to a contract must protect himself to the best of his ability; this does not mean at all that each is out to catch the other, but an undertaking is a serious matter and should not be lightly given, otherwise the individual's reputation will soon be in question, if he is not ruined.

In manufactured goods it is often possible to make definite promises as to specification, etc., but in other matters – for instance the quantity of hay to be delivered from a field – it may be impossible to be exact, and such difficulties can usually be overcome to everyone's satisfaction by careful wording of the relevant clause. The hay may be cut, and your experienced eye may estimate that it will yield 30 tons. Instead of giving your word to deliver 30 tons, you can say "all the hay in the Long Meadow to be delivered, and the quantity expected to be about 30 tons". This protects you if it turns out to be 23 or 34 tons.

On the reverse of most printers' quotations which I receive are printed the following conditions. These are good, from the seller's viewpoint, and therefore bad from mine, although, to be fair, were I a printer I would use them, because of the protection they give. I wrote to the British Federation of Master Printers asking for permission to quote them here, which they have graciously granted. Study the clauses carefully and observe how strongly protected the supplier is. Of course the customer could, if he wished, insist on the elimination of any of the clauses, provided he did so and got the printer to agree before he gave his order. Certain circumstances might arise where it was necessary for one's own protection to insist on one or other of these clauses being inoperative so far as a particular order was concerned.

Here are the conditions:

Conditions of Estimate

1. COST VARIATION – Quotations are based on the current costs of production and are subject to amendment by the printer on or at any time after acceptance to meet any rise or fall in such costs.

2. VAT – The printer shall be entitled to charge the amount of any VAT payable whether or not included on the quotation or invoice.

3. PRELIMINARY WORK – Work carried out, whether experimentally or otherwise at customer's request will be charged.

4. PROOFS – Authors' corrections, including alterations in style, and the cost of additional proofs necessitated by such corrections will be charged extra. Proofs of all work may be submitted for customer's approval, and in that event no responsibility will be accepted for any errors in them not corrected by him.

5. DELIVERY AND PAYMENT – (a) Delivery of work shall be accepted when tendered and thereupon or on notification that the work has been completed the ownership shall pass and payment shall become due.

(b) Should expedited delivery be agreed and necessitate overtime or other additional cost, an extra charge may be made.

(c) Should work be suspended at the request of or delayed through any default of the customer for a period of 30 days the printer shall then be entitled to payment for work already carried out and materials specially ordered.

6. VARIATIONS IN QUANTITY – Every endeavour will be made to deliver the correct quantity ordered, but quotations are conditional upon margins of 5% for work in one colour only and 10% for other work being allowed for overs or shortage, the same to be charged or deducted.

7. CLAIMS – Claims arising from damage, delay, or partial loss of goods in transit must be made in writing to the printer and the carrier so as to reach them within three days of delivery and claims for non-delivery within 28 days of despatch of the goods. All other claims must be made to the printer within 10 days of delivery.

8. LIABILITY – (a) The printer shall not be liable for indirect loss or third party claims occasioned by delay in completing the

work or for any loss to the customer arising from delay in transit.

(b) Where work is defective for any reason, including negligence, the printer's liability (if any) shall be limited to rectifying such defect.

9. STANDING MATTER – (a) Metal, film, glass and other materials used by the printer in the production of type, plates, moulds, stereotypes, electrotypes, film-setting, negatives, positives, and the like shall remain his exclusive property.

(b) Type may be distributed and lithographic, photogravure, or other work effaced immediately after the order is executed unless written arrangements are made to the contrary. In the latter event, rent may be charged.

10. CUSTOMER'S PROPERTY – Customer's property and all property supplied to the printer or on behalf of the customer will be held, worked on, and carried at customer's risk.

11. MATERIAL SUPPLIED BY CUSTOMER – (a) The printer may reject any paper, plates or other materials supplied or specified by the customer which appear to him to be unsuitable. Additional cost incurred if materials are found to be unsuitable during production may be charged.

(b) Where materials are so supplied or specified, responsibility for defective work will not be accepted by the printer unless this is due to his failure to use reasonable skill and care.

(c) Quantities of materials supplied shall be adequate to cover normal spoilage.

12. GENERAL LIENS – Without prejudice to other remedies the printer shall in respect of all unpaid debts due from the customer have a general lien on all goods and property in his possession (whether worked on or not) and shall be entitled on

the expiration of 14 days' notice to dispose of such goods or property as he thinks fit and apply any proceeds towards such debts.

13. ILLEGAL MATTER – (a) The printer shall not be required to print any matter which in his opinion is or may be of an illegal or libellous nature.

(b) The printer shall be indemnified by the customer in respect of any claims, costs and expenses arising out of any libellous matter printed for the customer or any infringement of copyright, patent or design.

14. PERIODICAL PUBLICATIONS – A contract for the printing of periodical publications may not be terminated by either party unless written notice is given as follows:

Nature of Publication	*Length of Notice* (given at any time)
Weekly) Fortnightly) Monthly)	13 weeks
Two monthly) Quarterly)	26 weeks

Nevertheless the printer may terminate any such contract forthwith should any sum due thereunder remain unpaid.

15. FORCE MAJEURE – Every effort will be made to carry out the contract but its due performance is subject to cancellation by the printer or to such variation as he may find necessary as a result of inability to secure labour, materials or supplies or as a result of any Act of God, War, Strike, Lockout or other labour dispute, Fire, Flood, Drought, Legislation or other cause

(whether of the foregoing class or not) beyond the printer's control.

16. LAW – These Conditions and all other express terms of the contract shall be governed and construed in accordance with the Laws of England.

NOTE: Clause 9 (a) above shall not affect the practice in the bookprinting trade whereby moulds, and plates produced from moulds, prepared at a publisher's request and paid for by him, are his property.

I shall make no further comment on these excellent conditions.

Another point to remember is that any clause in a contract which would make the other party or yourself break the law is not enforceable – that is, you cannot contract outside the framework of the current law of the land.

I will now draw up an imaginary contract between an author and a publisher, and later comment on the different clauses:

AN AGREEMENT made this *ninth* day of *September* in the year 19. . . . between *Mr William John Blask, of First Street, Watford, Hertfordshire, WA1 7YY,* (hereinafter called the Author) of the one part, and *Blank & Blank Limited* of *24 Terminus Road, London, WC2A 7UU* (hereinafter called the Publisher) of the other part.

IT IS AGREED between the Author and the Publisher as follows regarding the manuscript now completed and at present called "*Fun and Games*":

1. The Author assigns to the Publisher the copyright of the material under the terms of this Agreement and the right to publish it in book form throughout the world. In the event of

publication either in the United States of America or in a foreign language, it is understood that the Author shall receive 50% (fifty per centum) and the Publisher 50% (fifty per centum) of any royalties, profits or outright sum received for any licence to publish granted by the Publisher. It is further agreed that the Publisher shall not protect the copyright in the United States of America against piracy as he does not consider this worth the cost in view of the normally remote chance of such piracy.

2. It is expected that the first edition shall be large, publication to be as soon as possible, to be printed on good quality paper, bound in cloth (or imitation cloth), price expected to be £20 (twenty pounds) but left to the discretion of the Publisher; subsequent editions to be in the original form or in such other form or at such price as he may decide in relation to existing market conditions. The Author shall retain a copy of the manuscript for safety, which is to be delivered to the Publisher should he so request.

3. The Publisher shall submit to the Author proof sheets of the first edition and of subsequent editions, or, in the event of the Author's decease, to his Executors, and the work of careful revision shall be promptly carried out. Failing agreement with the Executors, the Publisher reserves the right to employ an outside expert and shall deduct the cost from royalties. It is understood that the cost of corrections, to the extent that this exceeds 10% (ten per centum) of the cost of composition, shall be met by the Author.

4. The Author warrants the Publisher that the said work is in no way a violation of any existing copyright and that it contains nothing obscene, objectionable, indecent or libellous and will indemnify the Publisher for any loss, injury or damage, including any legal costs or expense properly incurred by the

Publisher, in consequence of any breach of this warranty.

5. The Publisher shall pay to the Author a royalty of 10% (ten per centum) on the published price of any and every copy sold. On export sales the royalty shall be at half rate. If the book has to be remaindered at less than one quarter of retail price no royalty shall be payable on copies remaindered.

6. Should extracts be taken from the book, any monies accruing therefrom shall be divided between the Author and Publisher, the former receiving 50% (fifty per centum) and the latter the balance 50% (fifty per centum).

7. Should the book be allowed to go out of print for more than eighteen months, all rights herein granted shall revert to the Author after six months' notice is given in writing to the Publisher, without prejudice to any monies due.

8. The Publisher shall render to the Author an account during November in each year (or within three months thereafter) after the date of publication and the amount shown to be due in royalties shall be paid to the Author at the time such account is rendered. Should accounts and payments not be so rendered, this Contract shall be cancelled and all rights shall revert to the Author without prejudice to monies due.

9. The Publisher hereby agrees to distribute review copies of the said book and to give six voucher copies to the Author on publication.

10. The Publisher reserves the right to carry out minor editing.

11. As the Publisher expects to spend a considerable amount on publicity, he hopes that the Author will give him first refusal of any other work proposed by him in book form.

12. It is understood that no similar book shall be written by the Author and published elsewhere which could conflict with the sales of the aforementioned book during the life of this Contract.

13. It is agreed that the Author shall enable the Author or his accountant to have access to the sales record of the Publisher to verify the sales figures, should the Author so desire.

14. The rights and obligations under this agreement shall be binding upon the Author and Publisher respectively and shall belong to and be binding upon the personal representatives and assigns of the Author and the successors in title and assigns of the Author respectively.

15. The Publisher retains the right before publication, to amend or in extreme cases to cancel this Contract in the event of any Government action or interference which would make the completion of the undertaking impracticable.

AS WITNESS the hands of the parties this *ninth* day of *September* 19...

Signature of Author/Publisher
Signature of Witness
Occupation of Witness
Address of Witness

Comments
A copy of the contract is retained while the original is away to be signed by the author, his signature being witnessed. When the signed original returns, the copy, this time signed by the publisher and witnessed, is sent to the author for his retention. This is known as exchanging contracts and is often done in the publisher's office or the home of the author.

The contract given above is a simple one; obviously a manuscript which has not been written requires different wording, as do manuscripts which have to contain illustrations – questions such as who is to pay for the reproduction rights of photographs and so on should be dealt with in the contract and not left to "mutual agreement" as is so often done and which frequently ends in misunderstanding and disagreement.

CLAUSE 1 – By obtaining the copyright instead of merely the right to publish for a given number of years, the publisher is in a stronger position. The percentages to be divided in the event of overseas publication might be disputed by the author, but the publisher could defend himself on the grounds that but for his initial risk and expense the book would probably never be published abroad, and also he has considerable expense in trying to market the average book overseas. The U.S.A. is probably the most important market for British books but foreign language translations are important as well, and the remarks are merely inserted to prevent any misunderstanding. Possibly a well-known author with the likelihood of U.S. publication might wish his American copyright to be protected by a special process, which can be done, or some authors might refuse to grant U.S.A. rights.

CLAUSE 2 – Notice that the publisher does not commit himself to the size of the edition, nor to produce the book at an exact price. This gives him the chance to protect himself if conditions alter during the time taken for production; for instance, he might originally have intended to publish 5,000 copies, but before the final proofs are returned to the printer, a slump might have set in for the particular type of book, so that he could reduce the quantity to, say, 2,000 copies. He also leaves himself free as to future prices or format. The clause insisting on a copy for safety gives him real protection in the event of loss or damage to the original manuscript during the production stage. It is surprising how often fires occur in printing works, and in the absence of this clause the publisher might find himself seriously out of pocket.

CLAUSE 3 – The publisher protects himself against executors, who in such a matter can be unco-operative. Care is taken in the event of the author carrying out an unreasonable number of corrections; a specific figure is inserted (and it is probably wise as it saves argument).

CLAUSE 4 – An interesting clause because it is of doubtful legality, and possibly could not be enforced in law, since if, for example, libel is included in the book, the publisher and even the printer are legally responsible, as well as the author. But the clause probably has a deterrent effect on an over-bold author, and is a customary one.

CLAUSE 5 – The reason for the nil royalty if the book gets remaindered is because in this circumstance the publisher has lost badly on the book anyway.

CLAUSE 6 – Self-explanatory.

CLAUSE 7 and 8 – These, as can be seen, give good protection to both author and publisher. Always remember there are two sides to every contract, and the perfect contract from the viewpoint of one party would be unfair to the other, so all contracts are really a compromise, but *your* aim must be to secure all the safeguards you possibly can, and, as mentioned above, never promise what there is doubt about your being able to fulfil.

CLAUSES 9 and 10 – Self-explanatory.

CLAUSE 11 – Some publishers insist on first refusal of the next three books, while others request first refual of all future books. Personally, I prefer to hope the author will play fair, and I always feel that the more you try to tie him to you, the keener he will be to break away. Indeed, it is doubtful if such a clause could be enforced in law unless it was much more tightly worded to cover all sorts of matters such as royalty rate, advances, if any, and so forth.

CLAUSE 12 – This is self-protection for the publisher, but some authors will not agree to it except with modifications.

CLAUSE 13 – Often a customary clause in the publishing trade.

CLAUSE 14 – Protection for both sides, and necessary in a long-term contract such as the one under discussion.

CLAUSE 15 – An emergency clause for the publisher's protection. This clause is probably unnecessary, as I believe all contracts are subject to cancellation or alteration when something arises which can properly be termed "an act of God", or a cause of some kind beyond the parties' control.

Although the foregoing is a simple contract, several lessons can be learned from the care with which the clauses have to be drawn up.

Read, re-read, sleep on and think over all clauses in a contract – but do not forget no one can cover every possible combination of contingencies, and perhaps, with life so short, it is as well.

Giving Notice Under a Contract

Let us assume that the book referred to in the above has been allowed to go out of print for a period of over 18 months; what should the author do? In practice he would probably visit or write a friendly letter to the publisher to ask the position, and often such matters are handled in that friendly manner with excellent results.

Sometimes, however, an author meets with a "difficult" publisher; in other words, the one party to a contract may find he does not get on well with the other party, for some reason or other, and wishes to take advantage of the clause. When this occurs, things are less easy. If the other party is a small private partnership concern, a carefully worded letter, referring to the contract, giving its date and referring to the appropriate clause by number, would be sent by registered post to the senior partner with a request for acknowledgement. In the case of a limited company, the correct procedure would be to write to the Company Secretary. Something on the following lines would meet either case in our sample contract:

Dear Sir

I refer to our contract dated 9 September 19XX for the publication entitled "Fun and Games". I understand this book has been out of print for eighteen months, and I hereby exercise the option to terminate the said contract under Clause 7. Please treat this as the necessary six months' notice in writing requisite for the exercise of the said option without prejudice to any monies due to me. I shall thereafter consider myself free to arrange for publication elsewhere.

Please confirm termination of contract in accordance with this letter.

Yours faithfully

Non-Fulfilment of Contract

What happens if one party feels the other side has not fulfilled a contract? Normally, unless there is any clause to the contrary, a contract or agreement is enforceable in courts of law. What can be said, however, is that going to law on such a matter can be expensive and is rarely to be recommended. Quite often the hint of legal action will be enough to make the other party see reason, but remember it may be you who is being unreasonable; so many of us, when faced with our own problems, cannot see the other side's viewpoint. Damages awarded for a breach of contract may be heavy; amounts depend on what is involved.

In many trades a system of arbitration has been evolved when disagreement arises, so as to eliminate the cost of litigation; but like all substitutes for the real thing, the system has its faults. Among them is the fact that it is sometimes hard to find someone of knowledge, integrity and impartiality who is acceptable to both sides, if it is a case of appointing a sole arbitrator. If an arbitrator has to be appointed by each side, with an umpire, then costs are already running up. Since an arbitrator is within his rights in demanding his fee before announcing his verdict, the shock to the loser is frequently considerable, if slightly delayed.

On the whole, I think it is better to have an ordinary contract which can be taken before a court of justice if the need arises, but some may prefer the arbitration method. Where the latter is used, I think it only wise to include some precaution in the clause as a protection; for example:

> "Any dispute that shall arise between the parties hereto with reference to this Agreement or the construction thereof or any matter contained in or arising out of this Agreement shall be referred to two Arbitrators one to be appointed by each of the parties hereto or their Umpire in accordance with the provisions of the Arbitration Acts, 1889 and 1934, or

such statutory modifications or amendments thereof as shall for the time being be in force or alternatively at the option of either party, to be declared beforehand, recourse to normal Courts of Justice may be adopted."

Depending upon what is at stake, at least the option of going before a court is available. In practice, many will risk an arbitration, but if you insist on going to Court, if you have a good case, you will probably win a settlement out of court before the hearing starts. Few firms like the publicity of being sued.

Employment Agreements or Contracts

In the United Kingdom anybody who is taken on as an employee is entitled to receive a Contract of Employment under "The Contract of Employment Act, 1963", and subsequent legislation which includes the 1975 and 1981 Employment Acts.

This contract must give particulars of the terms and conditions of employment, as follows:

Rate of pay, dates on which pay is paid, and job title.

Normal hours of work and entitlement to lunch-hour and other breaks.

Holiday entitlement.

Procedure for making up pay during illness, if any.

Whether there is a pension scheme.

Length of notice of termination to which the employee is entitled. By law the entitlements are:

1. After four weeks' employment – one week's notice.
2. For each year of continuous employment between two and twelve years – one week's notice for each year.
3. For continuous employment of twelve years or more – twelve weeks' notice.

Procedure for taking up grievances and disciplinary

complaints.
Disciplinary rules.

Example of a Contract of Employment
In this statement under the Contracts of Employments Acts, XXX Company gives you, ... of ....
particulars of the terms and conditions on which it is employing you with effect from the ....

1. Your initial rate of pay is £...... per four-week month. You will be paid on the last Friday before April 5th each year and at four-weekly intervals thereafter.

2. Your normal hours of work are .... per week. Your daily hours are .... You are entitled to a one-hour mid-day meal break, 12.30 p.m. to 1.30 p.m. or at a different time by agreement.

3. In addition to Public Holidays and the other days on which the Office is closed at Christmas time, your holiday entitlement is three working weeks per calendar year. Dates are to be settled as far in advance as possible with the Manager. On the completion of three years' service, you become entitled to an additional one working week's holiday per year, provided that this latter is taken during the Winter months October to April.

4. In addition, the Directors always give favourable consideration to requests for extra holidays without pay.

5. EITHER
The Company will continue to make up your nomal pay during any unavoidable absence during sickness.

OR

The Company will pay you statutory sick pay in accordance with the law, provided that you comply with the Company's rules and regulations as regards the notification of such illness, and the provision of the necessary doctor's certificate, details of which are available from your Manager.

6. The Company does not provide a pension scheme.

7. You are entitled to receive one week's notice of termination after four weeks' employment; one week's notice for each year of continuous employment between two and twelve years, and twelve weeks' notice if the period of continuous employment is twelve years or more. You are required to give the Company one week's notice of termination, but longer if possible.

8. The title of your job is ....

9. Disciplinary rules: These are kept to the minimum, but the Company cannot employ those who break them.
   (a) You are not allowed to enter the premises outside working hours.
   (b) You are not allowed to smoke on the premises.
   (c) You are not allowed to use the Company's postage stamps for private purposes.
   (d) You are not allowed to use the fire hose for any purpose except putting out a fire.
   (e) You must ask the Manager's permission if you wish to:
      (1) make a private telephone call;
      (2) use the photocopier for private purposes;
      (3) purchase items of stationery, wrapping materials, etc.

(4) purchase stock;

and if permission is given, you must:

(i) be as brief as possible on the telephone;

(ii) pay for calls made or materials used or bought, at cost;

(iii) do private work only during the lunch hour.

10. If at any time you are dissatisfied with any disciplinary decision affecting you, you may make a complaint to any of the Directors who are in the Office at the time.

11. If you have any individual grievance relating to your employment here, the procedure is for you to raise it with the Manager. If you are still dissatisfied, the procedure is then for you to raise the matter with any of the Company Directors who are in the Office at the time.

Some employees may want complicated service contracts, which might be very difficult and expensive to break. I would advise strongly against these, initially at any rate. Give your employees the ordinary length of termination of notice as required by law, but no more.

At a later date, a loyal employee might feel he deserves a better service contract, but it should be considered later, rather than earlier.

Part-time Staff

The Act covers part-time staff provided that they work more than sixteen hours each week. However, part-time staff who have been continuously employed for more than five years are covered if they work more than eight hours per week.

Job Title

It is important to give careful thought to a job title. The consequences of a badly chosen title can be far reaching. For example, under the law, if a woman with more than two years' service, takes maternity leave, provision must be made for her to return to a similar, although not necessarily identical, position as she held before (although this does not apply to small employers).

INDEX

By the same author

GENERAL & SOCIAL LETTER WRITING

Covers all aspects of general and social correspondence.

A.G. Elliot gives practical advice about writing materials, style, layout, opening and closing, and letter-writing etiquette.

There's particular help on the writing of the more difficult letter, with examples of how to express sympathy, write references and compose job applications.

Uniform with this book

ELLIOT RIGHT WAY BOOKS
KINGSWOOD, SURREY, U.K.

In the same series

YOUR BUSINESS THE RIGHT WAY TO RUN IT

The complete guide to running your own business. Covers everything the self-employed or small businessman needs to know: the organisation of premises and equipment; tax and financial matters; recruitment and training of staff; legal aspects; costing and pricing; sales and publicity.

BOOK-KEEPING THE RIGHT WAY

The essential reference tool for the small businessman, the self-employed and the treasurer of any club or voluntary organisation. John Whyte-Venables explains the principles of correct book-keeping simply and in a logical sequence, showing how to prepare and present accounts for tax purposes.

Uniform with this book

ELLIOT RIGHT WAY BOOKS
KINGSWOOD, SURREY, U.K.

In the same series

THE RIGHT WAY TO IMPROVE YOUR ENGLISH

Not a dull, dry grammar book, but an elegant exposé of the errors which people so easily make, with explanations of how they arise.

Of equal benefit to the English and to the foreign student of English, this book gives a thorough grounding in all the basic elements needed to secure a polished and full command of the language.

HOW GOOD IS YOUR ENGLISH?

No matter how good you *think* your English is, there are bound to be things you do not know. Test your knowledge, in an enjoyable way, of: derivations, vocabulary, meanings, spellings, pronunciations, grammar, punctuation, literature and authors.

Uniform with this book

ELLIOT RIGHT WAY BOOKS
KINGSWOOD, SURREY, U.K.

In the same series

THE RIGHT WAY TO SPELL

It has a big horn on its nose, but is it a Rhino*ceros*? Rhino*sceros*? Rhino*cerus*? or Rhino*scerus*? Find out which is the correct spelling and, at the same time, discover the "rules" of spelling and how words are built up.

For teachers, parents, foreign students and typists alike, J.E. Metcalfe's book is the essential guide to the peculiarities of the English language.

MICRO-COMPUTERS FOR BUSINESS & HOME

The book for people who don't understand computers. Explains how to choose and use a computer, what the jargon means and how to write programs.

Whether your interest is in home or small business computers, Alan Fryer's book provides the ideal introduction.

Uniform with this book

ELLIOT RIGHT WAY BOOKS
KINGSWOOD, SURREY, U.K.

OUR PUBLISHING POLICY

HOW WE CHOOSE

Our policy is to consider every deserving manuscript and we can give special editorial help where an author is an authority on his subject but an inexperienced writer. We are rigorously selective in the choice of books we publish. We set the highest standards of editorial quality and accuracy. This means that a *Paperfront* is easy to understand and delightful to read. Where illustrations are necessary to convey points of detail, these are drawn up by a subject specialist artist from our panel.

HOW WE KEEP PRICES LOW

We aim for the big seller. This enables us to order enormous print runs and achieve the lowest price for you. Unfortunately, this means that you will not find in the *Paperfront* list any titles on obscure subjects of minority interest only. These could not be printed in large enough quantities to be sold for the low price at which we offer this series.

We sell almost all our *Paperfronts* at the same unit price. This saves a lot of fiddling about in our clerical departments and helps us to give you world-beating value. Under this system, the longer titles are offered at a price which we believe to be unmatched by any publisher in the world.

OUR DISTRIBUTION SYSTEM

Because of the competitive price, and the rapid turnover, *Paperfronts* are possibly the most profitable line a bookseller can handle. They are stocked by the best bookshops all over the world. It may be that your bookseller has run out of stock of a particular title. If so, he can order more from us at any time—we have a fine reputation for "same day" despatch, and we supply any order, however small (even a single copy), to any bookseller who has an account with us. We prefer you to buy from your bookseller, as this reminds him of the strong underlying public demand for *Paperfronts*. Members of the public who live in remote places, or who are housebound, or whose local bookseller is unco-operative, can order direct from us by post.

FREE

If you would like an up-to-date list of all Paperfront titles currently available, send a stamped self-addressed envelope to
ELLIOT RIGHT WAY BOOKS, BRIGHTON RD.,
LOWER KINGSWOOD, SURREY, U.K.